BUILDING HEALTH
COALITIONS
IN THE BLACK
COMMUNITY

Dedicated to health coalition facilitators everywhere

BUILDING HEALTH COALITIONS IN THE BLACK COMMUNITY

Ronald L. Braithwaite
Sandra E. Taylor
John N. Austin

Sage Publications, Inc.
International Educational and Professional Publisher
Thousand Oaks ■ London ■ New Delhi

For information:

Sage Publications, Inc.
2455 Teller Road
Thousand Oaks, California 91320
E-mail: order@sagepub.com

Sage Publications Ltd.
6 Bonhill Street
London EC2A 4PU
United Kingdom

Sage Publications India Pvt. Ltd.
M-32 Market
Greater Kailash I
New Delhi 110 048 India

Printed in the United States of America

Library of Congress Cataloging-in-Publication Data

Braithwaite, Ronald L., 1945–
    Building health coalitions in the black community / by Ronald L.
Braithwaite, Sandra E. Taylor, John N. Austin.
        p.   cm.
    Includes bibliographical references (p.   ) and index.
    ISBN 0-8039-7309-8 (acid-free paper)
    1. Afro-Americans—Health and hygiene.   2. Public health—United States—
Citizen participation.   3. Health promotion—United States—Citizen
participation.   4. Health planning—United States—Citizen participation.
    I. Taylor, Sandra E., 1955–   II. Austin, John N.   III. Title.
    RA448.5.N4 B73 2000
    362.1'089'96073—dc21   99-6715

00   01   02   03   04   05   06   7   6   5   4   3   2   1

Acquiring Editor:	Jim Nageotte
Editorial Assistant:	Heidi Van Middlesworth
Production Editor:	Diana E. Axelsen
Editorial Assistant:	Nevair Kabakian
Typesetter:	Lynn Miyata
Indexer:	Jeanne Busemeyer
Cover Designer:	Michelle Lee

Contents

Preface

The purpose of this book is to highlight issues pertinent to health coalition-building initiatives, particularly as they relate to African American communities. Coalitions, partnerships, alliances, and collaborative linkages designed to confront compelling health problems in African American communities have proliferated during the past 15 years. These efforts have provided a useful methodology for grassroots organizers, as well as health and human service providers, to address the lack of health promotion efforts and health equity in African American communities. Some argue that a thin line exists between individual responsibility and systemic barriers relative to the quality of life in these communities. Those on either side, however, would be hard pressed to deny the positive outcomes that can ensue from discussion on the topic. This book seeks to provide a forum for stimulating such discussions that are useful in coalition building for health promotion.

The book begins with an historical context for the deployment of coalition partnerships as a change strategy. The book also provides guidelines for those interested in using bottom-up planning approaches to improve the plight of disenfranchised groups. In this sense, it is intended as a resource for enhancing knowledge and understanding about the dynamics of community organization and development in the African American community.

The development of coalition partnerships has been shown to be a viable strategy toward solving various social problems. For example, a recent large-city effort of government, educational, and corporate entities involved the launching of new opportunities for the continued education of new teenage mothers. Countless other examples indicate the trend toward collaboration in combating existing and potential problems that plague America's communities. Particularly within the African American community, certain social problems—

crime, illiteracy, and unemployment are only a few—tend to have a disproportionate effect. Moreover, an array of health problems, including cancer, hypertension, drug addiction, HIV/AIDS, and violence, disproportionately affect this
population. Coalition partnerships have been viewed by different entities,
including the community residents themselves, as a needed strategy toward
alleviating human suffering in areas of preventable disease.

Although it is generally accepted by scholars, health care professionals, and
community residents themselves that coalitions hold the key for the development of African American communities, little information is available about the
organization of such collaborative efforts. This book attempts to illuminate this
situation and discusses guidelines for the development and sustenance of
coalitions in these communities. It presents a brief history of collaborative
efforts in African American communities and examines privately and federally
funded initiatives for health promotion. It also views coalitions in theoretical
and applied contexts. Coalition partnerships are discussed in conjunction with
the faith community, the combating of substance abuse, environmental threats,
and urban/rural settings. The effort borrows from our varied experiences as
directors, principal investigators, evaluators, and other roles with community
coalitions. It represents a compilation of archival data, oral history and anec-
dotes, case studies, survey research, and syntheses of parts of the current
literature in its development. The terms *coalition, partnership,* and *collaborative efforts* are used interchangeably to refer to the coordination of two or more
parties' efforts to attain a mutually agreed-on goal.

Acknowledgments

We would like to acknowledge the contributions of the numerous colleagues, especially Micky Roberts and Martha Boisseau, who provided conceptual feedback while this manuscript was in the initial phases of development. We also extend our sincere appreciation to graduate students Clark Denny, Leslie Fieldler, Johanna Leffler, Micah Milton, Arian Krause, and Golda Aliza Smith of the Rollins School of Public Health of Emory University, who generously provided their time in doing library research and contributed significantly to the refinement of the chapters herein. Meg Gwaltney of COSMOS Corporation and David Robbins from the U.S. Center for Substance Abuse Prevention also provided access to national data sets for the chapter on "Coalitions Combating Alcohol, Tobacco, and Other Drug Use." We are particularly grateful to Betty Stevens of the Rollins School of Public Health of Emory University, who contributed significantly to the editing, formatting, and final preparation of the manuscript for submission to the publishers. Finally, we are grateful to the Center for Substance Abuse Prevention (Grant #1 H86-SP03-221-01) for supporting parts of the programs and evaluations reported herein.

An Historical Analysis of Health and Collaborative Efforts in African American Communities

INTRODUCTION

In examining coalitions for health promotion in African American communities, it is important to place this focus in historical context. African Americans have had an ominous history with respect to health care and their general welfare in the United States. Prior to the Emancipation Proclamation and the ending of the War between the States (Civil War), the health and welfare of most African Americans were the responsibility of the property owners (slaveholders). It was economically advantageous to the slaveholders to ensure minimum levels of health and well-being for their "property" and to ensure that their "property" would be in a position to yield the greatest return for the investment (Trattner, 1989). As for free blacks, Trattner indicates that they were essentially forced to develop their own informal self-help mechanisms. Hence, religious institutions and fraternal organizations became important vehicles for freedmen to receive health care.

The dynamics of the aftermath of the Civil War were to shape health care and the general well-being of African Americans for years to come. In addition to the dislocation and impoverishment of southern states, thousands of freedmen had been cast into a situation for which there was no preparation. As Trattner (1989) indicates, these people were "largely uneducated, unskilled and unprepared for their abrupt change in status" (p. 78). Axinn and Levin (1992) reveal that at the conclusion of the war, the individual states gave first attention to the needs of veterans and their dependents for artificial limbs and cash pensions. Concern for the orphans of Confederate soldiers led to the establishment of orphanages and of apprenticeship procedures. As for the general white population, most southern states set up central public welfare stations for the distribution of food and clothing. The states moved to deal with the freed black population through attempts to re-institute a system of control of the labor market. (p. 88)

Black codes were passed and implemented in all but one of the southern states. These black codes restricted work opportunities, property ownership, and the commerce in which African Americans could engage. Axinn and Levin (1992) further indicate that African American youth who were under 18 years old or orphaned or whose parents could not support them were remanded to an apprentice program. Apprenticeships for African American youth, however, lacked the components provided for the white youth. Food, clothing, and education were not guaranteed components of apprenticeships, and preference for apprenticeships was given to the former masters. Obviously, there was more concern for controlling African Americans than for addressing issues of their health and general welfare.

The creation of the Bureau of Refugees, Freedmen, and Abandoned Lands (Freedmen's Bureau) in 1865 constituted the single most important organization that would eventually lay the foundation for the improvement of the health and welfare of African Americans in the United States. The bureau was situated in the federal War Department and charged with providing an array of services to both refugees and freedmen in the southern states (Summerville, 1983; Trattner, 1989). General Oliver O. Howard, a West Point graduate, was designated to administer the bureau. His appointment to this position was crucial to the future health and welfare of the freedmen. Summerville writes, "In General Howard's view, the most urgent want of the freed people was education" (p. 3). This notion, combined with General Clinton B. Fisk's (assistant commissioner for the bureau) desire "to place the former slaves in a position to help themselves" (p. 3), resulted in the development of initiatives that would provide the underpinnings for beginning to address the health and welfare needs of African Americans.

Axinn and Levin, Summerville, and Trattner assess the diversity and number of activities in which the bureau engaged to support and sustain the former slaves. The bureau initially focused its efforts on education. It moved from assisting freedmen to read and write to establishing schools and, eventually, colleges. The bureau's medical department provided treatment including hospitalization, and the bureau also established hospitals and orphanages to provide for the health and welfare of the freedmen.

Evidenced in the previous passages regarding the Freedmen's Bureau is that it was the paramount vehicle for laying the foundation for the health and welfare of African Americans. The orientation that the freedmen be able to help themselves, coupled with the emphasis on education, shapes the approach to health care and general welfare that characterized the history of African Americans in these areas. This chapter explores the history of health care and the general welfare of African Americans in the United States and focuses on hospitals, medical schools, and African American physicians as important areas for analysis.

HOSPITALS AND HEALTH CARE

Axinn and Levin (1992) indicate that the Freedmen's Bureau was successful in establishing 46 hospitals. It is reasonable to assume that the majority of these hospitals were founded primarily to serve the newly freed African American population. Although Axinn and Levin do not discuss the disposition of these hospitals further, it is also reasonable to assume that these hospitals predominantly served the freed African Americans while also serving the majority (white) population. Some of these hospitals served as the vanguard for the "black hospitals" that eventually emerged. Because these hospitals served a primarily African American population, however, many did not survive.

Carter G. Woodson (1934) notes that up until the 1930s, African American physicians established their own hospitals, privately or publicly, as a consequence of the health care needs in the black community. The inability of these doctors to gain access to practice their profession in white hospitals, as a result of racism, also constituted an impetus for them to start hospitals in their homes or offices. In some cases, municipalities paid fees to these doctors for serving the African American clientele, which tended to be poor and unable to pay for services.

Through the 1930s, the African American community received hospital health care through one of several approaches. Health needs were met in segregated black hospitals (Woodson, 1934). If these institutions were not available, then they would receive health care in segregated sections, wards, or floors of white hospitals (Smith, 1990). It appears that white physicians were not averse to providing health care to African Americans in these institutions when it served their purposes (Summerville, 1983; Woodson, 1934). More specifically, when this population's care translated into income for the hospital, the hospital served them, but typically in segregated environments. Moreover, when white medical students' training was threatened by not having an adequate population on which to learn and enhance their practical experience, hospitals were more invested in the health needs of this population.

But in all actuality, it was not the health needs of the African American population that appeared to drive the interest of the hospitals so much as the need for their students to have adequate numbers of patients on which to practice and learn. More recently, the gruesome report about body snatchers raiding slave graves 100 years ago for corpses to be used as cadavers for medical students at the Medical College of Georgia is evidence that racism transcends life and death for African Americans (Seabrook, 1998). Approximately 170 African Americans were subjects of this abuse by the medical establishment. The dissection of these corpses was a tight secret and illegal practice until the legislature passed the Georgia Anatomy Act in 1887. It comes as no surprise that in northern and southern sections of the country, numerous African Americans had their health needs attended to in segregated facilities within white hospitals.

It is clear that white hospitals provided care for African Americans—despite their motives. At the same time, however, several hospitals across the country were established to serve African Americans through monies provided by both whites and blacks. Woodson (1934) writes that several hospitals of this type were established during this period, such as the Lincoln Hospital in Durham, the Brewster Hospital in Jacksonville, the Pine Ridge Hospital in West Palm Beach, the Terrell Hospital in Houston, the Wheatly Hospital in Kansas, the Provident Hospital in Chicago, and smaller such institutions.

There were no significant changes in hospitals and how they provided care to African Americans up through the era of the civil rights movement. Health care in African American communities was provided through a segregated fashion when provided by institutions such as hospitals. Many immediate needs were addressed through midwives and home remedies when medical personnel could not be accessed, and when African Americans visited health care centers (similar to medical visits in many low-income areas today), their experiences tended to be cold and insensitive. As a product and consumer of a segregated health care system, one of the authors of this work recounts his experiences growing up in a rural county of Virginia during the late 1940s. The following recaps what it was like for a number of African Americans during this period.

I am told by my mother that I was delivered at home by Dr. Christian. The nearest hospital was 25 to 30 miles away. It was primarily a white hospital with segregated facilities for African Americans. Dr. Christian was a local white physician who provided medical services to the residents—both black and white—of this rural county. Several years later, my family relocated to Baltimore, Maryland. In this city, we lived near, or rather in the shadow of, Johns Hopkins Hospital. The neighborhood that we lived in at that time was segregated and predominantly working class. For medical and health care, many—if not most—in the community received care through the clinics of Johns Hopkins Hospital.

I can remember my mother taking us to these clinics for health care. These are not fond memories. The period was the late 1950s and into the 1960s. We would usually arrive at the clinic early in the morning, no later than eight o'clock. Typically, we did not return home until four or five o'clock in the evening or later. Consequently, a visit to the clinic for an illness was a daylong event. As I recall, the clinics were segregated, that is, the patients tended to be primarily African American. The professional staff of the clinic (doctors, nurses, interns, and medical students) tended to be white. Some, at times, were non-Americans. Although the staff tended to be professional and competent in their demeanor and ministrations, the environment and the climate were sterile and cold. This environment and mode of receiving health care I found unsatisfactory, and I promised myself that I would never use such impersonal and cold services when acquiring medical or health care for myself or my family.

Several years later, with the War on Poverty and President Johnson's Great Society, I had the opportunity to work as a high school student with the city's Neighborhood Youth Corps. Another high school student and I were placed to work in Johns Hopkins's Ear, Nose and Throat Department. Dr. Berlin, a white doctor and, I believe, the administrator for the department, served as our mentor. Dr. Berlin presided over our total orientation to the hospital. We toured every department during that summer and received an orientation to each of them. Dr. Berlin structured our experiences so that we could observe, engage in limited participation and assistance in clinical settings, and work with the staff engaged in research. This experience provided a totally different picture of the hospital and altered my perspective. But this was the mid-1960s, and the atmosphere and attitudes were changing in most arenas within the country.

Although this anecdotal account points to a differential treatment, it pales in comparison with the insensitivity (and even abuse) experienced by some African Americans in America's health care facilities. A more systematic account is provided by Smith (1990) in a comprehensive and provoking analysis of the integration of hospitals and nursing homes in the United States. He indicates that the Hill-Burton Act basically did nothing to change racial segregation and discrimination in hospitals. This federal program, beginning in 1946, spent approximately $2 billion and provided nearly 1 million hospital beds. Smith further indicates that the National Medical Association and the National Association for the Advancement of Colored People (NAACP) were the primary advocates for integration of hospitals and health care services. According to Smith,

The efforts to integrate health care facilities in the United States in the 1960s produced significant changes in the organization of health care. Acute-care hospitals in all regions of the country abandoned policies to provide racially segregated services. (p. 562)

A progression of events accelerated the equal access of African Americans to hospital care. The first such event was the Supreme Court's decision in *Brown v. Board of Education* (1954), which held that "separate but equal" was no longer acceptable. This decision had a dramatic effect on the country in general and African Americans in particular. It spurred the civil rights movement, which gave rise to an array of new organizations emerging to challenge the country to live up to the ideals as manifested in its founding documents—the Bill of Rights and Constitution—as well as the ideals that World War II was fought to protect. The activities of these organizations gave support to the passage of the Civil Rights Act of 1964. This provided added impetus to African Americans' equal access to hospitals in that the act stipulated that no one could be discriminated against because of race, color, or national origin by programs or activities receiving federal funding (Smith, 1990). If white hospitals received Hill-Burton monies and were in noncompliance, they risked losing substantial federal dollars.

The final event that accelerated African Americans' equal access was the 1965 passage of the Medicare and Medicaid legislation. Smith (1990) indicates that failure of hospitals to meet the antidiscrimination requirements of this legislation would mean that

(1) beneficiaries would be unable . . . to take advantage of their medicare entitlement, (2) the medical staff would lose a major source of income, (3) no funds would be available through the medicaid program to care for the indigent, and (4) the hospitals would face catastrophic financial loss. (p. 575)

These events shaped and altered the course of African Americans' access to hospitals.

At the same time that discrimination in hospitals was officially ending, a crisis was looming on the horizon for the 200 black hospitals that existed in the 1900s. Taravella (1992) indicates that by 1990, the number of black hospitals had dwindled to 8. To determine how many of these 12 black hospitals continued to exist and serve their respective communities in 1998, the authors conducted a telephone survey of the hospitals displayed in Table 1.1. This survey resulted in the verification of the continued existence of the 8 hospitals. As indicated in Table 1.1, the surviving 8 hospitals are Howard University Hospital, Meharry/ Hubbard Hospital, Newport News General Hospital, Norfolk Community Hospital, Richmond Community Hospital, Riverside General Hospital, SE Specialty Hospital (L. Richardson Memorial), and Southwest Hospital.

In addition to providing health care to the African American population, black hospitals served as training grounds for African American physicians, nurses, and other allied health care personnel. These institutions served persons who were poor and indigent when care was not available in the white hospitals.

TABLE 1.1 The 12 Remaining Black Hospitals in 1990

Hospitals	*City*
Howard University Hospital	Washington, DC
Meharry/Hubbard Hospital	Nashville, TN
Newport News General Hospital[a]	Newport News, VA
Norfolk Community Hospital	Norfolk, VA
Richmond Community Hospital	Richmond, VA
Riverside General Hospital	Houston, TX
SE Specialty Hospital (L. Richardson Memorial)	Greensboro, NC
Southwest Community Hospital and Medical Center	Atlanta, GA

SOURCE: Private, not-for-profit black-owned hospitals listed by the Coalition to Save the Black Hospital, January 1993.
a. Reorganizing under protection of bankruptcy laws.

The demise of the black hospitals is attributed to several factors: one-way integration, reduced federal funding, and skyrocketing health care costs.

As the United States enters the new century, the challenge to the remaining black hospitals is to adapt to the emerging trends of health care. The primary aspects of these trends appear to be managed health care and health maintenance organizations, with insurance playing a major role in who receives services; what those services will be; and when, where, and how the services will be delivered. In a market in which African Americans represent only 3% of health care providers (Whigham-Desir, 1994), the remaining African American-owned hospitals will have to strive to overcome racism, discrimination, scarce resources, and management challenges to continue to exist and serve the African American community.

MEDICAL TRAINING

Obtaining medical training has been just as difficult for African Americans as obtaining equal access to medical services in white hospitals. It is quite intriguing that, in 1890, there were 909 black physicians in practice (Woodson, 1934). This means that within a short 25 years after emancipation, African Americans— with meager resources and limited opportunities—had elevated themselves, despite astronomical odds, to the level of putting an impressive number of persons through professional schooling. An understanding of the training necessary to become a physician, however, must also be viewed in historical context.

During the early 20th century, medical training and education had not risen to the status and prominence they presently enjoy. An array of paths and schools with dubious credentials could lead to the acquisition of medical credentials. Abraham Flexner, an American educator, was employed by the Carnegie Foundation for the Advancement of Teaching to assess medical education in the United States (World Book, 1995). His 1910 report titled *Medical Education in the United States and Canada* declared that of 155 medical schools in the United States and Canada, only Johns Hopkins Medical School provided an adequate medical education. Further, the report raised questions regarding medicine's ability to meet the standards for being considered a profession. Of course, these findings led the medical field to respond with the development and implementation of standards that would raise the stature of the medical enterprise.

Even in 1890, the credentials of the 909 African American physicians were as good as the credentials of their white counterparts. Further, as the standards in the medical profession grew, so did the number of African American physicians in the United States. There were 1,734 African American physicians by 1900; 3,409 by 1910; 3,885 by 1920; and 3,805 by 1930 (Woodson, 1934). This number increased to 13,243 in 1980 and to 20,864 during the 1990s (U.S. Bureau of the Census, 1992). The majority of African American physicians received their training from African American schools. Howard University graduated 20%; Meharry Medical College, 28%; and Shaw University, 11%. Woodson indicates that Shaw University's medical program was closed in 1902 because it did not have adequate equipment to meet emerging medical school standards. The remaining African American physicians received their medical training from various medical schools including Harvard, Temple, University of Michigan, and Northwestern University. Quite revealing, however, is that these schools never graduated more than 3% of the African American physicians. Most of these schools seemed to produce from less than 1% to 3% of the African American physicians receiving formal training. Of course, the production of African American physicians at this rate was, and is, hardly adequate to manage the health needs of the African American community. Consequently, the importance of African American schools of medicine can be discerned. These were the only medical schools producing African American physicians in large numbers. Still, these numbers were not adequate to effectively serve the African American population of the United States. With the demise of Shaw University, there were only two African American schools with medical programs until much later in the century.

Presently, there are four African American medical schools in the United States. The Howard University Medical School and the Meharry Medical College may be viewed as the early pioneers in training African American physicians. These two schools have provided medical education and training for the majority of the African American physicians presently in practice.

Howard University was founded in 1867 by an act of the U.S. Congress (National Association for Equal Opportunity in Higher Education [NAFEO], 1988). According to NAFEO, Howard has the largest concentration of African American scholars and Ph.D.s of any institution of higher education. Howard's medical school has been producing physicians for more than 100 years. Its graduates have received numerous accolades in their professional practice and have alleviated considerable suffering among the African American population. A small representation of medical graduates who have achieved distinction includes W. Montague Cobb and Rudolph Fisher.

W. Montague Cobb earned his M.D. degree in 1929 (Robinson, 1978). Robinson indicates that Dr. Cobb was the champion and pioneer for black rights and equality in medicine and went on to serve as the president of the National Medical Association, the American Association of Physical Anthropologists, and the Anthropological Society of Washington. Dr. Cobb was also a prolific scholar, producing more than 500 monographs, editorials, and scientific papers.

Rudolph Fisher, on completing his internship at Freedmen's Hospital, began his medical practice in New York City. In addition to his medical talent, Dr. Fisher possessed talents in music and literature. Paul Robeson called on Dr. Fisher to arrange songs for his performance in New York. In literature, Dr. Fisher produced several memorable works that used satire to depict urban life. Several of his short stories were published in the *Atlantic Monthly* (Robinson, 1978).

In addition to the achievements of its graduates, Howard University's medical school has benefited from having distinguished faculty such as Charles Drew and Daniel Hale Williams. Robinson (1978) indicates that Charles Drew served as chief surgeon of the Howard Medical School. Dr. Drew is perhaps best known for discovering processes and procedures for preserving blood plasma. Daniel Hale Williams was brought to Washington in 1894 to reorganize the Freedmen's Hospital of Howard University. Dr. Williams pioneered radical heart surgery, and his fame and skill as a surgeon were widely known and respected.

The second most notable African American medical school, Meharry Medical College, was founded in 1876 as a medical department of Central Tennessee College and became an independent medical college in 1915 (NAFEO, 1988). Like Howard University's medical school, Meharry has been at the forefront of producing distinguished graduates and securing the best medical talent to provide medical training to its students.

The 1988 NAFEO directory describes Meharry, as cited by the Robert Wood Johnson Foundation, as a "national resource" for its role in educating minority health professionals. The directory notes that Meharry has trained nearly one third of the African American physicians and dentists presently engaged in practice. In addition, Meharry graduates constitute 40% of African American faculty in U.S. medical schools and 25% of the faculty in U.S. dental schools.

Of equal significance, Meharry graduates are providing health care in 46 states
and 22 foreign countries.

Charles R. Drew University of Medicine and Science, founded in 1966, and
Morehouse School of Medicine, founded in 1975, are the two newcomers in
preparing African American physicians. These schools have commitments to
research and clinical training that are firmly embedded in providing efficient
and effective services to the community, particularly the African American
community. Because there have never been enough African American physicians to serve the African American community, these two schools enhance the
capacity to develop and produce increased numbers of African American physicians who can serve their communities.

Nager and Saadatmand (1991) provide information on the white medical
schools that are producing large numbers of African American physicians. They
indicate that Michigan State, North Carolina, New Jersey, University of Illinois,
and Temple medical schools have 12% to 13% African American enrollment.
They also indicate that the University of California at Los Angeles, Cornell,
East Carolina, Hahnemann, University of Michigan, SUNY-Brooklyn, SUNY-
Buffalo, Pittsburgh, East Tennessee State, and Wright State medical schools
have 10% to 11% African American enrollment and that there are 16 medical
schools with an African American enrollment of 7% to 9%.

AFRICAN AMERICAN PHYSICIANS

In considering the health care of African Americans, it is a logical progression
to move from a discussion of the situation with medical schools to a discussion
of African American physicians that they produced. As previously noted, at the
time of emancipation and the end of the Civil War, there were hardly adequate
numbers of African American physicians to provide for the health needs of the
African American population. Segregation and discrimination subsequent to
this period played a significant role in affecting the plight of African American
physicians. Historically, there has been difficulty in accessing a medical education. Nager and Saadatmand (1991) and Summerville (1983) detail many of the
issues in this respect. Aside from the obstacles of discrimination and racism for
some populations, the cost of medical education has also posed a serious
impediment. In addition, limited opportunities to acquire training at appropriate
sites contributed to the problem of access to practice for the African American
physician.

As presented in the discussion on hospitals, few African American doctors
had professional status to practice their professions in white hospitals until the
civil rights movement. The National Medical Association was created primarily
because African American physicians were excluded from membership in local
constituent medical societies of the American Medical Association (Smith,

1990). Exclusion from local medical societies meant that physicians would not have hospital privileges, because hospital privileges were based on standing in these societies.

The evolution of the *Brown v. Board of Education* decision, the civil rights movement, the Civil Rights Act, and the Medicaid and Medicare programs marked a change for African Americans and African American physicians. The emphasis in the United States and in health care changed from one of exclusion to one of inclusion. African Americans seeking medical care were received in predominantly white facilities with little or no overt discrimination. Similarly, African American physicians gained access to the American Medical Association and its local societies with less overt discrimination and also gained access to hospital privileges in what had previously been white hospitals. African American medical students also gained "easier" access to the nation's medical schools.

Despite these gains, Nager and Saadatmand (1991) indicate that a shortage of minority health care providers looms on the horizon, although the nation will experience a surplus of doctors for the next two decades. Further, they indicate that although African Americans compose 12% of the population, "they constituted only 7.8% of first-year medical students for 1987 to 1988 in the United States and only 6% of the total enrollment in U.S. medical schools" (p. 788). Nager and Saadatmand indicate that of 15,830 medical school graduates for 1986-1987, only 820 were African American. Ten years later, there were 1,153 African American first-year medical students (Association of American Medical Colleges [AAMC], 1997). There were 5,303 African American students enrolled in U.S. medical schools. Finally, the AAMC indicates that there were 15,923 medical school graduates for the 1996-1997 academic year, of which 1,158 were African American. These numbers indicate the challenge that lies ahead in increasing the presence of African American physicians in the health care arena.

Although a shortage of African American physicians is projected by Nager and Saadatmand (1991), Whigham-Desir (1994) has expressed concern about the impact of health reform in the 1990s on the practice of African American physicians and health institutions. She identifies managed care, solo versus group practices, and health maintenance organizations as challenges that will have to be addressed by African American physicians if they are to survive with the reforms that are presently occurring in the health care arena.

Health care for African Americans in the United States has always been tenuous at best. Receiving medical services and acquiring the knowledge, skills, and sanction to practice medicine have remained a constant challenge to African Americans. Unfortunately for African Americans and for physicians who have provided care, the mortality and morbidity rates have been consistently higher for this group than for the white population. Despite this dynamic, there have been gains noted in life expectancy and general health. These gains, however, have been less dramatic than for the white population. Morbidity rates are still relatively high, but they are lower than in previous decades.

Although African Americans have gained greater access to health care, this access has not yet necessarily translated into better health. Substantial contributors to continued poor health are diet and lifestyle. Health education and health promotion are viable strategies for combating this situation. These strategies, however, will require collaboration between hospitals, physicians (particularly African American physicians), and medical schools to design and deliver these approaches in a professional and culturally sensitive manner. If appropriately executed, this collective approach holds an abundance of promise. The history of collective behavior in the African American community shows that a variety of successful activities have been launched using this approach. The following section highlights some of these partnerships.

COLLABORATION IN
AFRICAN AMERICAN COMMUNITIES

Aside from collaborative efforts for health promotion in African American communities, a number of cooperative initiatives have historically existed toward facilitating overall life chances. The history of collaborative efforts and cooperative initiatives in African American communities can be traced to the late 1700s with the development of the Free African Society, founded in Philadelphia in 1787 (Estell, 1994). The Free African Society, noted as the first African American organization in the United States, was a catalyst for the creation of the African Methodist Episcopal (AME) and AME Zion Churches in 1816 (Jacques, 1992). The Free African Society and the churches worked closely together in promoting social cohesion and economic and medical aid to poor blacks. Similarly, the abolitionist movement of the 19th century produced many organizations concerned with African American issues. These included the American Colonization Society (founded in 1816) and the New England Anti-Slavery Society (founded in 1833). Although most of the organizations were dominated by whites, numerous African Americans played major roles in the movement and the organizations that evolved (Estell, 1994).

In 1865, Congress created and empowered the Bureau of Refugees, Freedmen, and Abandoned Lands, which became known as the Freedmen's Bureau (Axinn & Levin, 1992; Trattner, 1989). The bureau was unique in that it helped repair the damages of the Civil War for the needy in the South regardless of race or wartime loyalties. Second, it became the first federal experiment that dealt with the provision of human resources. Under the auspices of General Oliver O. Howard, the bureau provided a variety of services to African American and white southerners (Axinn & Levin, 1992). These services included functioning as (a) a health center where doctors were employed and hospitals were maintained to reduce the mortality rate, (b) an employment and settlement agency, and (c) an educational center that encouraged the funding of African American schools and universities. The bureau also served as an agency that assisted with legal and civil rights advice and advocacy (Karger & Stoesz, 1990).

In 1875, more than 1 million African American farmers organized the Colored Farmers' Alliance in union with the populist Grange movement (Day, 1997). Other unions formed were the Knights of Labor (1869), Working Women's Protective Union (1894), and the National Colored Labor Union (1869).

Many black organizations came into existence during the late 19th and early 20th centuries, the majority of which were geared toward education, social betterment, and religious training. In 1895, the National Medical Association was founded to further the interests of black physicians, pharmacists, and nurses. The National Association of Colored Women was created in 1896 to reinforce the social welfare activities of black churches, fraternal orders, other women's clubs, and mutual benefit societies (Trattner, 1989). The National Negro League was formed in 1900 to promote commercial development. The common thread to all of these organizations was the realization by African Americans of the benefits of joining together and joining with others to gain improvements in their conditions.

The cooperative initiative of the Niagara Movement marked a turning point in collaborative efforts of the African American community. The movement, spearheaded by W. E. B. Du Bois in 1905, demanded enfranchisement, education, and race-based distinctions. In 1901, the Niagara Movement became known as the National Association for the Advancement of Colored People (NAACP). The original founding of this organization began with three white individuals—William English Walling, Mary White Ovington, and Henry Moskowita (McKissack & McKissack, 1991). Mary Ovington attended the 1905 meeting of the Niagara Movement as a reporter and experienced the conditions in the African American ghettos of New York City. She, in alliance with Walling and Moskowita, and after enlisting the support of African American leaders, proposed that a conference be held to discuss full citizenship rights for African Americans, public recognition of African American contributions to America's stability and progress, and the renewal of the struggle for civil and political liberty (Estell, 1994). Founders of this organization felt that existing tactics for African American advancement neglected issues of civil and political rights and reflected too moderate a position on economic issues.

In addition to conducting lobbying efforts and publicity campaigns, the NAACP soon established a legal redress committee. Its legal activities included responses to white violence against African Americans, such as legal defense and resistance to the extradition of African Americans accused of interracial violence. Several cases supported by the NAACP reached the Supreme Court, such as *Buchanan v. Wharley* and *Moore v. Dempsey*. The case of *Buchanan v. Wharley* held unconstitutional municipal ordinances requiring residential segregation; the case of *Moore v. Dempsey* overturned the conviction obtained of an African American in a mob-dominated proceeding (Tushnet, 1987). These cases, and other activities associated with the courts, strengthened the NAACP's commitment to obtaining and solidifying the political and civil rights of African Americans. The NAACP soon emerged as the first African American coalition with the expertise and finances to fight for justice on behalf of the African American community in U.S. courts and legislatures.

The NAACP's greatest victory was won in 1954 when the U.S. Supreme Court renounced the separate but equal doctrine in the *Brown v. Board of Education* of Topeka, Kansas, decision. This decision, which eliminated segregation in public education, overturned the Supreme Court's prior ruling in *Plessy v. Ferguson* (1896), which had legalized the doctrine of separate but equal treatment for African Americans.

In the post-civil rights era, the NAACP focused its attention on a number of growing problems and issues within the black and white communities, such as teenage pregnancy, drug abuse, infant mortality, and unemployment. Today, the NAACP is considered the oldest civil rights organization in the United States. It is categorized as a fraternal, advocacy, social, and political-educational organization that serves as a model for many groups that advocate for social change (Estell, 1994).

During the early part of the 20th century, several other organizations concerned with the plight of urban African Americans emerged. In 1906, blacks and whites met for the purpose of studying the employment needs of African Americans. This group, known as the Committee for Improving the Industrial Conditions Among Negroes in New York, studied the racial aspects of the labor market (particularly the attitudes and policies of employers and unions) and sought to identify opportunities for qualified African Americans. At the same time, the League for the Protection of Colored Women was established to provide similar services for black women relocating from the South to New York and Philadelphia. In 1910, the Committee on Urban Conditions Among Negroes was organized. A year later, the organization merged with the Committee for the Improvement of Industrial Conditions Among Negroes in New York and the National League for the Protection of Colored Women to form the National Urban League (Jacques, 1992). The Urban League was composed of white social workers, and, in coalition with other groups, it was concerned with helping rural African Americans adjust to urban life. This led the organization to provide aid in housing, job training, health, recreation, education, and employment. In the 1960s, the Urban League began to emerge as a force in the civil rights struggle (Eagles, 1986).

Collaborative efforts in African American communities continued when Franklin Roosevelt took office in 1933. He developed the plan that came to be known as the New Deal. The New Deal created programs of relief, recovery, and reform for citizens of the United States. Hungry people were fed, housing was built for the homeless, and hospitals and health centers were established for the sick, the disabled, and the aged. Trade unions played an important role during this period for African American and other races. The African Americans' first significant contact with the trade unions occurred when the Congress of Industrial Organizations began to unionize the large manufacturing, transportation, communication, and service industries in the 1930s.

After World War I, large numbers of African Americans migrated to the cities from the rural South. Especially in centers of the steel and automobile industries (cities such as Pittsburgh, Detroit, and Chicago), African American workers joined white immigrants working in the factories and manufacturing plants. This situation was the first instance of massive racial integration in the workplace (or elsewhere) in the history of the United States (Jacques, 1992). As the unions organized in these industries, their success depended on their ability to unite workers of all races and nationalities in support of the goals of unionism.

In 1951, the National Negro Labor Council fought against discriminatory hiring practices in companies. It collected petitions, held conferences and demonstrations, and supported strikes, and its representatives spoke out on radio and television. One of its leading advocates was Paul Robeson, the civil rights advocate who published a monthly newspaper titled *Freedom*. This newspaper became the instrument of the Negro Labor Council. Another prominent trade union leader of this period was A. Phillip Randolph, who was the organizer and leader of the Brotherhood of Sleeping Car Porters. The Brotherhood was to be the first nationwide organization for African American workers, and Randolph became the major voice for African Americans in general within decision-making centers of the country's labor movement.

Other organizations such as the Congress of Racial Equality (CORE), Leadership Conference on Civil Rights, Southern Christian Leadership Conference, and the Student Nonviolent Coordinating Committee (SNCC) were formed during this period. CORE was organized in 1942 by James Farmer to confront racism and discrimination. One of its chief activities was organizing sit-ins and freedom rides throughout the South. CORE began to challenge segregation in restaurants, swimming pools, and municipal facilities in northern and border states. Its first sit-in was staged at a restaurant in the Chicago Loop. From Chicago, the organization spread to other cities and other causes. CORE also played a key role in the southern voter registration drives from 1962 to 1964. The organization was instrumental in the wave of demonstrations that swept the South during the spring and summer of 1963. CORE, more than any other organization, was responsible for the massive outpouring of direct action against housing, employment, and education discrimination in the North.

The Leadership Conference on Civil Rights was founded in 1950 in Washington, D.C. This organization was responsible for coordinating campaigns that resulted in the passage of legislation such as the Civil Rights Acts of 1957, 1960, and 1964; the Voting Rights Act of 1965; and the Fair Housing Act of 1968 (Estell, 1994).

Young people in the South became increasingly active in demonstrations and sit-ins. There was little organization among these students, however, until 1957 when Ella Baker, a graduate of Shaw University and long-time civil rights activist, organized a Southern Christian Leadership Conference for youth. Attended by 200 delegates from southern communities in 12 states, the conference subsequently met monthly to coordinate student demonstrations across the South. In 1960, the Southern Christian Leadership Conference became the Student Nonviolent Coordinating Committee (SNCC) and organized demonstrations across all colors, ages, and income lines with the ideals of nonviolence and passive resistance.

In 1957, a Civil Rights Act was passed and signed into law. This legislation called for the establishment of a special Civil Rights Division within the Department of Justice. There were several other provisions of the Civil Rights Act, including the creation of a Federal Civil Rights Commission that was charged with studying the status of civil rights and making recommendations for legislation. The commission was authorized to intervene in cases involving violations of civil and voting rights (McKissack & McKissack, 1991). These gains in civil rights are directly attributable to the coalitions and collaboration occurring between a number of organizations and groups within American society.

Since 1954, there have been organized efforts by both African Americans and other races to secure equal rights and opportunities for African Americans. Wide-ranging civil rights legislation has been passed protecting rights in areas such as housing, voting, employment, and use of public transportation and facilities. The civil rights movement of the 1960s mobilized African Americans and other races. People were jailed or lost their jobs in defiance of Jim Crow laws. Homes and churches were destroyed, and massive riots, maimings, and murders occurred during this turbulent time. Because of these devastating occurrences, nearly 250,000 African Americans and whites assembled in 1963 on the grounds of the Lincoln Memorial in Washington, D.C., to express concern about the passage of civil rights legislation. Civil rights bills had been sent to Congress, but southern congressmen used filibusters to prevent action on several important pieces of legislation. The organization and leadership of the civil rights groups strategized to pressure Congress into passing the legislation with limited debates and filibustering. The March on Washington was a cooperative effort of several civil rights organizations including the Southern Christian Leadership Conference, CORE, the NAACP, the Negro American Labor Council, and the National Urban League. Cooperation by these organizations led to the success of the March on Washington and ultimately contributed greatly to civil rights gains in the country.

Through demonstrations, sit-ins, and marches, the movement of the 1960s aroused widespread public indignation, thus creating an atmosphere in which it was possible to make positive changes in America. For example, in 1967, the National Urban Coalition was founded to improve the quality of life for disadvantaged persons in urban, predominantly African American, communities. This organization pursued its mission through the combined efforts of business, labor, government, and community leaders (Estell, 1994).

During the 1960s, minorities were becoming more aware of the benefits of organizing and of their potential as participants in various organizations. In the mid-1960s, African American curricula materials were, for the most part, inaccurate, insensitive, and inadequate. Few stories portrayed the African American experience with depth and understanding. Although schools were integrated, curricula and textbooks excluded the contributions of African Americans, women, and other minorities. Educators, parents, and students began verbalizing their concerns about the lack of representative cultural materials. The concept met with overwhelming resistance by opponents who feared that accommodating a multicultural curriculum would result in lowered academic standards. Through persistence, school districts were convinced that multicultural education was the best approach and that cultural diversity was a strength. School administrators imparted their needs and concerns to publishers and universities. These entities in turn began publishing more representative material and making multicultural education courses a part of teacher certification. The struggle of African Americans for civil rights encouraged and inspired other minority groups to also seek social justice relative to their causes. Organizing, forming coalitions, and collaborating became primary tools for addressing social issues by many disenfranchised groups.

Primary health issues that have faced the African American community from the mid-1970s through the 1990s include teenage pregnancy, violence (particularly among African American males), and substance abuse. Recent strategies employed to arrest or ameliorate these problems include mentoring programs, "boot camps," and rites of passage programs. Again, what each of the primary strategies has in common is collaboration among multiple stakeholders committed to achieving positive change. African American communities are becoming partners with court systems, police departments, city governments, and social and human service programs. The lessons of the past have taught that the issues facing the African American community, as well as the community at large, are complex and dynamic. Further, no single individual or organization has a definitive solution. Therefore, the community must come together with all its stakeholders to evolve a dynamic and integrated plan to address these salient issues.

2

The Federal and Foundation Emphasis on Coalition Initiatives

SIGNIFICANCE OF FEDERAL AND FOUNDATION EMPHASIS ON COALITION INITIATIVES

The current federal and foundation emphasis on coalition initiatives reflects the belief that collaboration is essential to effective community development to affect the pervasive social and health disparities that exist in the African American community. The development of coalitions of agencies, institutions, and community members that focus on disease prevention and health promotion initiatives is currently increasing in popularity as an intervention aimed at strengthening the social fabric (Butterfoss, Goodman, & Wandersman, 1993). Throughout the United States, the Center for Substance Abuse Prevention has funded more than 250 community partnerships, each for 5 years, with the goal of reducing morbidity and mortality caused by alcohol and other drugs (Goodman & Wandersman, 1994).

In the mid-1980s, the Centers for Disease Control and Prevention (CDC), in partnership with state and local health departments and community groups, began the Planned Approach to Community Health (PATCH) process. The five elements considered critical to this process are that (1) community members participate in the process, (2) data guide the development of programs, (3) participants develop a comprehensive health promotion strategy, (4) evaluation emphasizes feedback and improvement, and (5) the community capacity for health promotion is increased (CDC, 1993d).

Federal government agencies and private foundations are increasingly turning their support to community-based coalition partnerships (Eisen, 1994). These coalition partnerships, created to address national health problems, exist at the community level and include community-based organizations (Scarlett,

Williams, Kenneth, & Cotton, 1991). Currently, these agencies and foundations invest millions of dollars in these partnerships for health promotion interventions (Butterfoss et al., 1993).

The World Health Organization (WHO, 1989) indicates that the working committee for guidelines for the development of a national AIDS prevention and control program should include the representation of all important sectors and organizations. Included among these are health, education, social, and counseling services; religious, insurance, legal, and political bodies; communications media; nongovernmental organizations; and research institutions. This approach may be applied to the communication of information not only for the prevention of HIV but also for overall health promotion and disease prevention interventions.

FEDERAL EMPHASIS

The federal government supports a substantial number of contracts with non-profit organizations. It provides significant contributions for the increased presence of these organizations within the community (Smith & Lipsky, 1993). This section will focus on examples of federally funded initiatives through the Office of Minority Health (OMH), the CDC, and the Center for Substance Abuse Prevention. These initiatives establish major grant programs that are designed to support community-based coalition partnership programs.

Office of Minority Health

The U.S. Department of Health and Human Services (USDHHS) established the OMH in 1985. The office provides leadership throughout the departments of the USDHHS by establishing, coordinating, and advocating policies, programs, and activities for the improvement of the health of minority populations. These populations include African Americans, Asian Americans, Hispanics/ Latinos, Native Americans, and Pacific Islanders.

According to Audrey F. Manley, M.D., M.P.H., former acting deputy assistant secretary for minority health and former acting surgeon general, the mission of the OMH is "to improve the health of racial and ethnic populations through the development of health policies and programs" (USDHHS, 1985, p. 1). The *Report of the Secretary's Task Force on Black and Minority Health* documented a persistent, distressing contrast in key health indicators among certain subgroups of the population. The report identified six causes of death that collectively accounted for more than 80% of the excess mortality shown among African Americans and other minorities. These causes were cancer, cardiovascular disease and stroke, chemical dependency, diabetes, homicide and accidents, and infant mortality.

The USDHHS created the OMH to target the health-related conditions responsible for most of the excess mortality suffered by racial and ethnic minority populations. These include alcohol and other drug use, cardiovascular disease and stroke, cancer, diabetes, infant mortality, violence, and HIV/AIDS.

Moreover, the OMH focuses on many issues essential to health improvements including access to health care, cultural competency in health service delivery, improved health data, and the availability of health professionals to serve minority communities. The OMH is dedicated to advancing minority health through public-private partnerships. The emphasis on coalition partnerships includes systematic consultation and joint projects with the heads of Public Health Service agencies, minority health coordinators of these agencies' state and local entities, and national and community-based organizations. The OMH expands the minority health network of state and local government officials and other professionals to include community-based organizations and consumer advocates that promote community, family, and individual action to improve the health status of minority populations. The OMH starts activities to achieve this expansion and includes the following strategies:

● Link federal and state minority health contacts with local government and private sector counterparts with consumers and community-based organizations that work with minority populations.

● Encourage the establishment of minority health entities in each state.

● Help participants in the network seek complementary funding from other public and private sources and leverage the funds available for their programs.

● Collaborate with 16 historically black colleges and universities to develop a comprehensive, community-based, model program, the Family Life Center, to prevent violence among minority males. Family Life Centers conduct community needs assessments and work with other community groups and other historically black colleges and universities to develop prevention and intervention strategies. They also develop coalitions to execute these strategies (OMH, 1995).

Since 1986, through its Minority Community Health Coalition Demonstration Grant Program, the OMH has worked with minority communities to deal with diabetes and other health problems. Sample descriptions of such demonstration projects follow.

Black Health Care Coalition of Kansas City

The Black Health Care Coalition of Kansas City, Missouri, is one of the OMH-funded diabetes projects. This coalition targets the Kansas City area's high concentration of African Americans who are at increased risk for diabetes-related health problems (OMH, 1995). Staff screen people in five local churches for diabetes and diseases with similar complications.

During its 3-year span, the coalition reached approximately 7,000 community members. People in the community who received screening were directed to obtain health care. The staff conducted follow-up care by telephone and letters encouraging the participants to return if they had blood sugar, hypertension, or cholesterol problems. A nurse visited community members who did not return despite their health problems. Many program participants stated that the program was their only form of health care.

Project Health

In 1992, Project Health received one of 15 grants awarded by the OMH under the Minority Community Health Coalition Demonstration Grant Program. The goal of Project Health is to improve the overall health status of African Americans who reside in the Inner City North of Milwaukee. The initial strategies implemented include enhancing the advocacy capability of the Black Health Coalition to effect system change and providing prevention education programs, information dissemination, and community organization on chemical dependency, violence, cancer, cardiovascular diseases, and health care access.

Saturday Institute for Manhood, Brotherhood Actualization (SIMBA)

Currently, the SIMBA program, partially sponsored by the OMH, addresses problems relating to the high death rate among young African American males caused by injury and other health-related issues. Based in Atlanta, Georgia, SIMBA is a consortium consisting of the Wholistic Stress Control Institute, the Lorenzo Benn Youth Development Center, and 10 other community organizations. Evaluation of the program indicates a decrease in violent behavior for participants. In February 1995, the USDHHS (1995b) cited SIMBA as an exemplary program in its report *Prevention: 1993 and 1994 Federal Programs and Progress: Healthy People 2000.*

Centers for Disease Control and Prevention

Among the centers of CDC is the National Center for Chronic Disease Prevention and Health Promotion. Its mission is "to prevent death and disability from chronic diseases, promote maternal, infant, and adolescent health, and to promote healthy personal behaviors" through partnership with health and education agencies, major voluntary associations, the private sector, and other federal agencies (CDC, 1999). Prevention, facilitated through education to effect behavioral change, must include close partnerships between the public health and medical care systems and the citizens of the United States.

American Red Cross-Centers for Disease Control Partnership

Scarlett et al. (1991) describe a public and private partnership between a community-based, national nongovernment organization, the American Red Cross (ARC), and a federal agency, the CDC. These organizations work together to initiate community responses to local health problems. The CDC funded the ARC to provide a communication program to inform and educate the public, members of racial or ethnic minorities, and youth about HIV infection and AIDS.

Results of this partnership include improved coordination of HIV and AIDS information and education efforts and increased community participation, with ARC expanding local public health efforts. The ARC-CDC partnership demonstrates how a comprehensive program for communication about HIV prevention can integrate into an existing national network necessary for the implementation of such a strategy. Moreover, the ARC-CDC collaboration is an example of how the private and public sectors can address a critical health issue in a process that enhances the effectiveness of each partner.

Project DIRECT

The CDC targets patients, health care professionals, and the public to receive diabetes information. The CDC's diabetes control programs provide leadership in creating new strategies and effective programs to reduce the complications associated with and resulting from diabetes. Coordinating efforts with all parts of the health care community, the CDC's diabetes control programs provide interventions through health systems and community-based approaches. State health departments in 40 states and territories run more than 150 programs. The types of programs range from technical assistance to social action programs.

Diabetes is more prevalent in racial and ethnic minorities than in whites in the United States (OMH, 1995). Therefore, the CDC initiated a demonstration project in 1990 called Diabetes Intervention: Reaching and Educating Communities Together (Project DIRECT) in the African American community of Raleigh, North Carolina. The goals of Project DIRECT, which took effect in October 1994, are to increase community awareness of diabetes and its risk factors and appropriate management; create accessible, acceptable intervention opportunities within the community; build grassroots capacity to implement and sustain health-promoting interventions; and facilitate more effective interactions between people with diabetes and their health care providers (OMH, 1995).

According to the CDC, Project DIRECT is a model for community-based diabetes prevention and control programs for urban minority communities, particularly African American communities. Directors of the project include community leaders, people with diabetes, members of the health care system, community-based organizations, and state and local health departments.

Diabetes Today

Through a partnership of state and local health departments, local community leaders and groups, and the CDC, the Diabetes Today program prepares health professionals and other diabetes advocates to develop and implement community-based diabetes programs. The staff from the CDC's Division of Diabetes Translation conducted a 4-day intensive course focusing on community assessment; selection of target groups, priority problems, and goals; planning of intervention strategies; and evaluation of the established program. This course prepared participants to direct their own 2-day courses with community leaders who will carry out local interventions. Funded by OMH, seven major community-based programs participated in the training sessions.

Center for Substance Abuse Prevention

The Center for Substance Abuse Prevention supports and promotes the continued development of community, state, national, and international comprehensive prevention systems. According to its mission statement, the center's goal is to connect people and resources with innovative ideas, strategies, and programs designed to encourage creative and effective efforts aimed at reducing and eliminating alcohol and other drug problems in our society. Many of the center's prevention efforts are community based. According to the center, the potential exists for comprehensive, coordinated, coalition-based strategies (USDHHS, 1994d). Its prevention programs and models are developed specifically for the local community. Interventions include broad-based community involvement and enhanced public and professional awareness of prevention.

Community Partnership Demonstration Grant Program

This community partnership program supports the formation of public-private sector partnerships in individual communities throughout the United States in their development of comprehensive programs for substance abuse prevention. The Center for Substance Abuse Prevention states that by bringing together all significant local agencies, organizations, and individuals concerned about alcohol and other drug abuse into a local partnership, it will develop a coordinated, long-term, communitywide approach.

This community partnership program, which began in 1990, supports grants to communities to establish effective community coalitions of organizations representing parents, schools, businesses, industry, and professional organizations in the development and implementation of comprehensive prevention programs. The program provides funding to communities to develop long-term approaches that meet the needs of their locality. The establishment of a variety of broad-based community alcohol, tobacco, and other drug prevention activities is the result of the partnership program. Furthermore, partnership efforts have developed and contain the internal stability necessary to address the prevention needs of their communities.

The conceptual framework of the partnership program encompasses and operationalizes community empowerment. The program is designed to demonstrate the potential for (a) expanding the scope and base of existing, well-developed partnerships programmatically, geographically, or both and/or (b) enlisting partnerships to join in forming a coalition in their current area to address substance abuse (USDHHS, 1995a).

FOUNDATION EMPHASIS

A foundation, according to the Foundation Center (1993), can be defined as a private, nongovernmental organization that assists other nonprofit or welfare associations primarily by providing grants for their social, charitable, or educational activities. Coalition-building efforts for community health empowerment include programs of several philanthropic foundations (Braithwaite & Taylor, 1992). The commitment of private resources is required for health promotion and disease prevention initiatives at the community level. Private partnerships with community-based organizations are becoming increasingly important, especially those partnerships that include sustainable efforts (Scarlett et al., 1991).

W. K. Kellogg Foundation

Communities and community partnerships are an integral part of the W. K. Kellogg Foundation's grant-making strategy. The primary function of this foundation is to help build the capacity of individuals, grassroots organizations, and institutions to respond to needs and to create positive change in their communities.

FIRST

An example of the W. K. Kellogg Foundation's focus on community as a base is the For Individuals Recovering Sound Thinking (FIRST) initiative. In fiscal year 1992-1993, the foundation provided a grant of $100,000 in the African American community of Dorcester, Massachusetts, to reduce the spread of gang violence by providing peer counseling and leadership to at-risk youth.

Kellogg Youth Initiatives Program

The Kellogg Youth Initiatives Program (KYIP) is a long-term commitment by the W. K. Kellogg Foundation to assist Michigan communities in addressing the needs of youth. The primary goal of KYIP is to improve the quality of life for young people by strengthening positive environments in which they can best develop and grow. In the interests of youth everywhere, a second goal is to create program models that may be adapted by other counties, cities, and regions throughout the United States.

KYIP involves a partnership between the W. K. Kellogg Foundation and selected communities willing to make a commitment of human and financial resources. Although the foundation continues its work with other state and national youth projects, KYIP is targeted specifically within Michigan at a section of urban inner-city Detroit, Calhoun County (largely a rural area with small towns and the city of Battle Creek), and the remote counties of Alger and Marquette in the state's Upper Peninsula. The communities identify youth-related needs and present proposals to the Kellogg Foundation to meet those needs. The foundation then reviews the proposals and makes grants to projects compatible with program objectives.

Grants are made for projects designed and operated by local groups and institutions. Projects center on the following innovative efforts: to improve local schools, expand preschool programs, involve youth in programs to assist senior citizens, provide recreation and job training for teens, improve housing, establish nutrition education, create alternative programs for school dropouts, and others.

The emphasis is on collaborative efforts. For example, youth organizations, churches, and schools might design a series of recreational programs to help build self-esteem among youth. The possibilities of KYIP are extensive, and collaboration is essential.

Comprehensive Approach

The communications project leader for the W. K. Kellogg Foundation stresses the importance of grant applicants seeking a comprehensive, holistic approach to community problems. Coalitions that include participation from a broad range of community leaders and institutions and that engage as many of them as possible to address a community problem are more likely to receive funding. During the 1990s, the W. K. Kellogg Foundation funded numerous capacity-building coalition partnership programs that linked universities, communities, and local health departments through their community-based public health initiative.

Robert Wood Johnson Foundation

Established in 1972, the Robert Wood Johnson Foundation is a national philanthropy and the largest foundation devoted to health care in the United States. The foundation concentrates its grant making in the following areas: ensuring access to basic health services, improving the way services are organized and provided to people with chronic health conditions, promoting health and preventing disease by reducing harm from substance abuse, and seeking opportunities to help the nation address the problem of escalating health care costs. According to the Robert Wood Johnson Foundation, in collaboration with the Henry J. Kaiser Family Foundation, partnerships and collaborations among different types of organizations are helpful in dismantling sociocultural barriers by generating a wider range of perspectives and resources. For example, community-based organizations can help identify barriers perceived by the community and develop solutions, service providers can implement changes that will reduce barriers, and universities and others bring a capacity for evaluation and research.

Opening Doors

The Robert Wood Johnson Foundation's Opening Doors program is intended to stimulate and assess promising approaches that increase access to maternal, child, and reproductive health services by reducing sociocultural barriers. In the Opening Doors context, maternal, child, and reproductive health services are primary care services for women of reproductive age and their children. The two types of projects that receive funding are (1) service projects to develop and test creative approaches to overcoming sociocultural barriers and (2) research projects to increase knowledge about sociocultural barriers and how they can be addressed. The Opening Doors program provides funding for projects that strengthen the ability of organizations to reduce sociocultural barriers by developing partnerships and collaborations among community groups, service providers, and universities.

Fighting Back

Fighting Back is a comprehensive substance abuse program operating in 14 communities throughout the United States. The Robert Wood Johnson Foundation has provided more than $45 million during a 7-year period to plan and implement innovative, communitywide initiatives. The goal of Fighting Back is to demonstrate that by consolidating resources and creating a single communitywide system of prevention, early identification, treatment, and aftercare, communities may reduce the demand for and use of illegal drugs and alcohol.

Project 3000 by 2000

Project 3000 by 2000 is an effort by the Association of American Medical Colleges to increase the number of underrepresented minority students entering U.S. medical schools each year. The target is 3000 students by the year 2000. The Health Professions Partnership Initiative, cosponsored by the W. K. Kellogg Foundation and the Robert Wood Johnson Foundation, challenges educators in medical, nursing, and other health professions schools to join together and then partner with local school systems and colleges. The goal of the initiative is to enhance the academic preparation of minority students and to nurture their interest in health careers, thereby increasing minority participation in all health professions, including medicine and public health.

Ford Foundation

The goals of the Ford Foundation include the following: to strengthen democratic values, to reduce poverty and injustice, and to advance human achievement. In its publication *Current Interests of the Ford Foundation: 1994 and 1995,* the Ford Foundation (1994) reported,

> A fundamental challenge facing every society is to create political, economic, and social systems that promote peace, human welfare, and the sustainability of the environment on which life depends . . . [and] the best way to meet this challenge is to encourage initiatives by those living and working closest to where problems are located; to promote collaboration among the nonprofit, government, and business sectors; and to assure participation . . . from diverse communities and at all levels of society. (p. 4)

The Ford Foundation supports urban collaboratives that strengthen community development. The collaboratives are composed primarily of local, private, public, and corporate funders. Furthermore, the Ford Foundation has turned to the formation of partnerships with other organizations. These organizations are public and private, and national and local. There are many examples of partnerships from this foundation, including the National Community AIDS Partnership, which works with community foundations and other local donors to sponsor preventive education and innovative services for people with AIDS; the Pittsburgh Partnership for Neighborhood Development, which is supported by foundations and corporations and provides financial, technical, and training assistance to neighborhood development organizations; and the Local Initiatives Support Corporation, a financial intermediary supported by a consortium of corporations and foundations (Ford Foundation, 1994).

The foregoing accounts of federal and foundation interest in supporting coalition partnerships are merely a small sample of such initiatives. Several other federal agencies with a direct or indirect impact on health status include coalition initiatives as part of their funding portfolios. These include programs in the National Institutes of Health, the National Institute of Justice, the Department of Health and Human Services, the Department of Housing and Urban Development, and the Department of Education, to name a few. Similarly, other large foundations not mentioned in this chapter that makes grants available for coalitions, partnerships, and collaborative include the Kaiser Family Foundation, the Rockefeller Foundation, the Gannett Foundation, the Mott Foundation, the U.L. Kaufman Foundation, the Josiah Macy, Jr. Foundation, the MacArthur Foundation, the Mason Charitable Trust, and the Pew Charitable Trusts, to name a few. Programs identified in this chapter appear to highlight the commitment of both the federal government and foundations to the use of partnerships as a viable methodology for fostering community health change and capacity building. By most accounts, employing coalition partnerships as an intervention is a strategy whose time has come.

3

Coalitions in Theory and Practice
The Urban Context

This chapter discusses coalitions that have developed for health promotion in the context of urban communities and their accompanying dynamics. In contrast to examining coalitions that have some other goal as the primary focus (e.g., education or business development), this chapter highlights those alliances that have evolved in the arena of overall wellness and morbidity reduction. This broad categorization includes an array of programs from violence prevention and teenage pregnancy to cancer awareness and recreation for older persons. The chapter also examines the role of coalitions in a discussion of their structure and functions in theoretical context and in practical application.

The health promotion coalitions discussed in this chapter were identified on the basis of their incorporation of varied partners. Although some coalitions are successful with a limited number of partners, it appears that with multiple partners, the chance of reaching the coalition's goal is improved. Hence, rather than including coalitions that include representatives from the business sector, the educational sector, and government, the selected coalitions discussed here include all the foregoing in addition to other representatives. Typically, representatives from the media, law enforcement, and the religious community, minimally, are part of community coalitions in many urban areas. These coalitions, then, appear to be some of the larger and more diverse organizations that function in the black urban community.

This chapter borrows from the published literature on coalitions in the African American community as well as from our extensive experiences in working with coalitions in urban areas. (A focus on rural coalitions and substance abuse prevention is presented in Chapter 7.) In light of the plethora of problems that beset the African American community (including HIV/AIDS, drug abuse, teenage pregnancy, and black-on-black crime), it is not surprising that coalitions have developed in response to this urban dilemma. Although these problems are found also in rural America, the density that characterizes cities makes the urban setting more intense. The various other characteristics that are typical of large cities also exacerbate the problems confronted by the African American community. For example, the impersonal environment of urban areas (in contrast to the more intimate relationships that tend to occur in rural settings) fosters concerns that are self-serving. The "village" concept, wherein persons look after one another, is virtually foreign. Instead, individuals are caught up in their own existence, and the welfare of their neighbors is not necessarily a priority. In addition, inner cities are characterized by a hetero-geneous populace. Although the heterogeneity of cities in and of itself is not necessarily problematic, such diversity can preclude the development of a feeling of community. Urban areas are also distinguished by transience, an indicator often associated with adversity. At a minimum, the transient nature of cities works against the building of stable and enduring relationships.

In response to the problems facing African Americans in cities, the develop-ment of coalitions appears to be a viable strategy in combating these maladies. Because coalitions exist to achieve goals that promote the welfare of its constituents, and because various pressing problems currently plague urban America, it seems logical that coalitions represent an appropriate response to this dilemma.

Coalition work in various black movements and organizations is apparent when analyzing certain activity, both in the historical and the contemporary contexts (as has been shown in Chapter 1). As discussed in the beginning of this book, there are many examples of coalition work throughout the history of African Americans. Much of the organizing of coalitions in the black commu-nity occurred in response to agreed-on problems confronting African Ameri-cans. Some of the work of coalitions emerged, however, as African Americans perceived victory to be eminent in their fight for certain resources. This latter situation points to the role of environmental conditions that play an important part in the formation of coalitions. Staggenborg (1986) explains that when there are indications that victory is possible, there is a greater incentive for the organization to combine resources, despite any differences that individual partners might have. Although her research focused on coalition work in the pro-choice movement, findings are relevant to many of the coalitions that have developed in the African American community. Specifically, Staggenborg's conclusions are especially relevant to the urban alliances discussed in this chapter. For example, she discusses the importance of external funding of coalitions for the alleviation of tensions. This point is particularly crucial for the maintenance of coalition work in the African American community. Given the economic disparity between black and white communities, African Americans are more dependent than their white counterparts for the sheer basics in everyday life. Hence, external funding better ensures that specific tasks of the coalition will be carried out.

Staggenborg's (1986) second point, that coalitions are more likely to succeed if they include established organizations (which are in a position to provide internal support and an organizational infrastructure that facilitates the interaction of coalition members), is equally important in the life of coalitions within the African American community. Coalitions are stronger when they include stable partners. Many of the coalitions studied for this book attest to the advantages in partnering with older entities. Among these advantages are physical resources such as office space and personnel to help with the development of the coalition. Still another important advantage is the credibility offered the coalition by an association having longevity. Such can be parlayed into additional external funding.

Staggenborg's (1986) final point, that coalitions are more likely to succeed if they focus on specific tasks (such as lobbying) that are too expensive for any one organization, is also important to the life of coalitions in the African American community. It can become easy for a coalition to be diverted in light of competing problems confronting the African American community. A focus on a single issue, however, solidifies the group and promotes a "consciousness-of-one." As such, reaching the coalition's goal becomes more attainable.

The application of the foregoing points taken from a study of the pro-choice movement, a majority white organization, to selected coalitions in the African American community appears appropriate. Perhaps this is due to the broadness of Staggenborg's (1986) points. For whatever reason, it appears that health promotion coalitions in urban environs would benefit from the foregoing just as other disparate causes have benefited. Other research notes similar characteristics that are important to the sustaining of coalitions. This chapter highlights some of the defining points of coalitions that have been presented in the literature in a discussion of their importance for the success of coalitions in the African American community.

Other authors have corroborated the importance of the points identified by Staggenborg (1986) to the development and maintenance of coalitions. Although these points may have been made within the context of a variety of issues and by various alliances extolling a host of concerns and conditions, their reiteration in the literature conveys the importance of each point for the viability of any given coalition. These points also allude to coalition building as a process involving appropriate links at appropriate times.

In a discussion of linking bridges between the fields of medicine and nursing, Chavigny (1988) highlights the importance of the process of coalition building. These steps are delineated as follows: (a) Know the interprofessional environment, (b) identify potential collaborators, (c) identify a common goal, (d) build credibility, and (e) link members of the coalition. Chavigny's discussion illumines the important point that although there is a wide range of partners from which a given coalition can choose, certain partners should invariably be included. This has relevance for the African American community, given the record of those entities that have historically supported the community's uplift and thus can be viewed as likely fits. A specific focus on nursing and its development with alliances for ensuring optimal health care provides an appropriate illustration. Chavigny makes the important point that although allies other than medicine could well be included, it would be shortsighted to develop the coalition void of the medical sector. Collaboration between the two fields of medicine and nursing is important because both are crucial to health care delivery. Depending on the nature of the coalition, certain partners should not only be included but also be given integral roles to carry out.

This chapter includes a focus on various urban coalitions with which we have worked during the past decade. It seeks to identify key elements in an examination of the nature of a coalition. It also discusses the development and maintenance of externally funded coalitions that have functioned in several inner cities in the United States. The coalitions are discussed within the frame of commonly accepted practices for the success of coalitions. Dluhy (1984, 1990), for example, provides a checklist of *dos* and *don'ts* for the development and maintenance of coalitions.

MOBILIZING AFRICAN AMERICANS FOR COALITION BUILDING

Given the health disparities affecting African Americans in America's cities, it is not uncommon for health professionals to identify needs peculiar to this population. Subsequently, various programs targeting specific problems have been developed within the black community. Whether sponsored by foundations, corporations, or local, state, or national government, these programs have varying degrees of success within the community.

In the development of coalitions for health promotion or in the realm of some other health-related field, black health care professionals, as well as community laypersons, play important roles. Russell (1992), for example, shows how nurses can serve as catalysts in initiating positive change within the black community. Via a case study method and a theory of social change, she examines the role of the nurse in community activism within the public policy arena. Not only are implications for the nursing profession unveiled, but more important to this discussion, she demonstrates that coalitions can be strengthened (and thereby reach targeted objectives) through active exchange between the various partners.

To further the cause of health promotion, black health care professionals must deliver in ways consistent with their levels of expertise. Studies show that African American professionals typically do their part in contributing to the black community. The issue of time is a reality, however, that prevents the impact that perhaps could be. Anyone who has dealt with coalition building is poignantly aware of the time that is expended. Indeed, coalitions require a great deal of time, in large part because of the discussions alone emanating from the goals and objectives of a given coalition. As Dr. Pat Kaye Edwards of the Mott Foundation has stated (personal communication, May 15, 1996), coalitions take time to be effective primarily because of a focus on "talking through" issues, rather than "talking about" issues. Consequently, communities are able to redefine problems in more holistic terms, to see one another differently, and to have a better map of the communities' resources.

Just as the health care professional within the African American community must contribute to the healthy development of the community, so do all persons residing within the community. Each person is a stakeholder, and each person must contribute if the coalition is to succeed. A commitment must be made, whether in time, funds, or some other effort. The coalition in an inner-city community can be a powerful asset if it has the full commitment of its constituents.

COALITION FORMATION: FROM THEORY TO ACTION

The study of coalitions from a theoretical and conceptual framework occupies much of the published research on the topic. In political and sociological theory, as well as in organizational theory, there has been a relatively large focus on coalitions and/or coalition formation. Cobb (1991) discusses coalition formation within the simulated context of a formal organization and concludes that the process of coalition formation involves a much wider range of concerns, objectives, and interconnected behaviors than suggested by previous research. His study points out the potential benefits of interpretivist research as an alternative to more traditional methods in the study of coalitions. Stevenson, Pearce, and Porter (1985) discuss the concept of coalitions in organization theory and research, pointing out that much of the research on coalitions is limited because of the "muddled" use of the term. Although clearer definitions have been found in studying coalitions in more recent years, there continues to be a lack of consistency in the operationalization of the term. Building on organizational theory, Gamson (1961) provides a statement of conditions and assumptions regarding coalition formation from a sociological perspective. Apart from the development of theory that denotes Gamson's study, of interest is some history about coalitions that is given, namely, that the subject of coalitions has been treated by historians and journalists for centuries. In this sense, the current barrage of interest in coalition development is not novel but instead an extension of much earlier foci directed at the utility of the coalition concept.

Cobb (1991) also points out that the definition of coalition continues to be problematic, despite years of use in research and theory. An aspect of the concept of coalition that has seen continuity in both historical and contemporary contexts is the characteristic of *power.* It appears that regardless of the context in which the concept is discussed, there is consensus that coalitions can be viewed as groups that hold the capacity to wield power or authority. In this sense, despite the range of differences definitionally, there is consistency in the view of coalitions as potential power brokers.

Several of the coalitions studied within the African American community provided examples of *power brokering.* One of the most vivid involved one coalition member who served as the president of the neighborhood association within a low-income neighborhood. This person was thought of as a natural leader by community residents, mainly because of a reputation for standing up to city hall and other giants that tended to be controlling forces in the lives of the residents. Because of the respect that she had commanded historically for her hard-nosed approach, and because of her ability to get things done, her name was synonymous with the coalition. Hence, whenever the coalition needed something (en route to accomplishing objectives), it depended on her to deliver. Similarly, politicians depended on her for delivering support. Because she was well aware of this, she effectively manipulated politicians and would-be politicians alike in obtaining services and resources for the neighborhood.

The manipulation of people and things in pursuit of community resources can be described as an art. Some people are quite adept at this, whereas others readily acknowledge that persuasion is not their forte. Regardless of the particular coalition members involved in selling their communities and causes, it is important that it is done by someone. Also important is the approach or the specific methods and techniques used in selling the community or cause. Dluhy (1990) identifies two types of sells—the hard sell and the soft sell. He describes the hard sell as a straightforward but threatening approach to political action. The hard sell approach involves backhanded tactics that seek to pressure one into submitting to the cause.

The soft sell, on the other hand, can be described as a more indirect approach. In this latter approach, "one uses persuasion, appeals to values, plays to the decisionmakers' sense of rationality, and often appeals to loyalty and friendship" (Dluhy, 1990, p. 79). The first tactic can be said to rely on brawn, the latter more on brain (particularly as defined as psychological persuasion). Most authorities on coalition building, including Dluhy, recommend that the soft sell be used whenever possible and that the hard sell be used only when all else fails. Because the development of allies, rather than alienation, is a key aim of coalitions, the effect of a hard sell is often negative, especially in the long run. If immediate action is the objective, however, the coalition may believe that it has to rely on what would normally appear to be a pushy and callous technique.

Whether the coalition seeks to garner funds or shape public policy, studies readily acknowledge the influence of coalitions in promoting causes and accessing commodities. Regardless of whether the approach is soft or hard, the influence of coalitions within the African American community is evident.

In addition, much has been discussed regarding the influence (and potential influence) of coalitions in the improvement of certain health conditions. The coalitions that we have studied during the past decade primarily tried to promote some specific aspect of improved health; simultaneously, they sought funds to supplement or continue efforts. For example, one coalition in Atlanta, Georgia, sought to prevent drug use/abuse among youth but also appealed to prospective donors for funds to bolster their primary funding source. Another coalition, also in Atlanta, pursued the prevention of teenage pregnancy as its main objective; it was successful in its attempts to obtain commitments for continued funding on exhaustion of its initial budget. In both cases, the coalitions carried out their objectives of promoting a specific health cause while tapping into new sources of funds for the programs' continuation. Neither of these coalitions, however, was involved in affecting policy or had as an objective the changing of law in advancing its individual agenda. Affecting policy and other long-standing objectives can be viewed as the real challenges to urban coalitions. Unlike African American coalitions in rural areas, African American urban coalitions tend to have larger numbers of partners. Consequently, a different set of issues prevails. For instance, children's after-school activities and parents' transportation patterns differ by geographical location. Thus, the planning of any given health intervention with the same objectives might well differ in its strategies depending on whether it is executed in an urban or a rural environment.

In several of the urban coalitions studied within recent years (including programs to prevent substance abuse), a popular component is after-school programs designed to deter youth from vices through the development of enhanced self-esteem and aspiration. Although this type of component might include liaisons with the local YMCA/YWCA and/or Boys and Girls Clubs in urban areas, collaboration with neighborhood churches might better characterize programs in rural settings. In this sense, there are more vehicles to achieve the desired goal in urban areas. This contributes to a wide variety of activities made possible by access to city living. The aforementioned coalitions in urban environments targeting youth are able to include visits to nearby museums, parks, and other recreational centers, as well as trips to professional sports events, all at a cost considerably lower than what could be done in rural areas. Ready access to such activities does not mean that the urban coalition's goals will be more easily achieved than those of the rural coalition. Although the variety may elude rural areas, the richness of popular activities in these areas is evident, and creativity abounds. Health and community fairs, Kwanzaa celebrations, and sports teams formation are popular activities designed by many rural coalitions as interventions. Many of these that we have observed have been excellently executed, and evaluation reports show that they are immensely enjoyed by participants. The more overriding question of their effectiveness, however, has not been unequivocally answered. On average, our data show inconsistent findings. Similarly, existing studies on interventions of this type are inconsistent. Needed are more rigorous longitudinal studies, especially those that compare interventions by type and geographical area (i.e., urban versus rural settings).

One of the issues that coalition members in urban settings often lament is the scrutiny accorded by researchers. Because members tend to recognize the role of the evaluator (often, as a consequence of orientations provided at the outset), evaluators are more likely to be accepted. Not so easily accepted, however, are researchers carrying out surveys and graduate students from nearby universities. Urban coalitions often have as their membership low-income persons, and these groups become popular samples for research. However, these historically targeted persons are becoming more resistant to surveys and to being researched at all. This can be seen in the increases in incentives once provided and now often demanded by prospective respondents. In addition, the proximity of many universities and other research facilities to low-income areas exacerbates the infiltration of these populations with surveys and other measurements. On the basis of our observations of these situations, we could say that urban residents have become savvy in inquiring about just reciprocity for their participation.

One final issue regarding urban coalitions, compared with rural, is that the former have a much wider and ethnically diverse community. Meeting the needs of urban communities involves a different set of dynamics. The urban coalition might consist not just of black and white partners but also of Hispanics, Asians, and other ethnic groups. This brings about an agenda that tends to make for a more complex setting than in rural areas.

The urban coalitions in various African American communities with which we have worked have generally followed a common set of guidelines. Although some coalitions have been more effective in moving from one stage to the next than have others, they all have sought to follow recommendations by funding agencies and/or experts in the area of coalition and partnership development. In this sense, the coalitions have had the potential for growth. Given that the development and maintenance of coalitions require a blueprint for greatest effectiveness, the coalitions started with a high probability of success. The success of any coalition (as discussed in Chapters 8 and 9), however, is directly related to the tenacity of the work groups and leaders.

4

Coalitions Combating Alcohol, Tobacco, and Other Drug Use

INTRODUCTION

Alcohol, tobacco, and other drug (ATOD) use has devastating effects on African American communities. Large numbers of people smoke, drink alcohol, or use illicit drugs, and although recent data suggest that the prevalence of ATOD use is declining, the numbers are still alarming. In 1994, more than 48 million people smoked, 110 million used alcohol, and 12 million had used an illicit drug (USDHHS, 1994b). Much progress is needed to achieve the *Healthy People 2000* objectives (Table 4.1) to reduce the use of these harmful substances and the associated health risks.

The difficulty of eliminating substance abuse and tobacco use is related to the complex, multiple factors that contribute to the behavior. The traditional health promotion emphasis on changing the individual's behavior to eradicate or reduce health problems has proved unsuccessful. The recent trend in health promotion evokes a socioecological understanding of ATOD use in which the locus for change is on the contextual factors that contribute to or enforce unhealthy behaviors, as well as on the individual. Drug and tobacco availability, norms surrounding use, advertising by the alcohol and tobacco industries targeting youth, the willingness of health care providers to give prevention or treatment counseling, and economic deprivation can influence an individual's decision to use substances. Therefore, prevention programs must be comprehensive in scope to address the multiple factors at the individual, family, community, and national levels that promote ATOD use (Wandersman et al., 1996).

TABLE 4.1 Selected Healthy People 2000 Objectives for Tobacco, Alcohol, and Illicit Drug Use

---

Tobacco

3.1   Reduce coronary heart disease deaths to no more than 100 per 100,000.

3.1a   Reduce coronary heart disease deaths among blacks to no more than 115 per 100,000 persons.

3.2   Slow the rise in lung cancer deaths to achieve a rate of no more than 42 per 100,000 persons.

3.3   Slow the rise in deaths from chronic obstructive pulmonary disease to achieve a rate of no more than 25 per 100,000 persons.

3.4   Reduce cigarette smoking to a prevalence of no more than 15% among persons aged 20 or older.

3.4d   Reduce cigarette smoking to a prevalence of no more than 18% among blacks aged 20 and older.

Alcohol and Other Drugs

4.1   Reduce deaths caused by alcohol-related motor vehicle crashes to no more than 8.5 per 100,000 persons.

4.2   Reduce cirrhosis deaths to no more than 6 per 100,000 persons.

4.2a   Reduce cirrhosis deaths among black men to no more than 12 per 100,000 persons.

4.3   Reduce drug-related deaths to no more than 3 per 100,000 persons.

4.4   Reduce drug abuse-related hospital emergency department visits by at least 20%.

SOURCE: USDHHS (1994a).

Coalitions have been described as state of the art in public health for complex problems such as substance abuse because they can plan and implement comprehensive multipronged interventions (Wandersman et al., 1996). This advantage has made coalitions and partnerships an increasingly popular response to the ATOD crisis in African American communities. This chapter will examine the coalition as a tool to reduce and to prevent ATOD use. Specifically, we will characterize ATOD use in African American communities, describe prevention models, and review the literature on the development and evaluation of ATOD coalitions. Although the aspects of coalition building, functioning, and evaluation may not be unique to coalitions dealing with substance abuse, the review is limited to literature dealing with this topic. A case study of ATOD coalitions targeting African American communities funded by the Center for Substance Abuse Prevention will also be presented to illustrate the concepts discussed.

THE SCOPE OF THE PROBLEM

Tobacco

Tobacco use is the number one preventable cause of premature death in the United States (USDHHS, 1994c). Health effects of tobacco use, particularly cigarette smoking, include lung, oral cavity and pharynx, esophageal, and larynx cancer; coronary heart disease; and chronic obstructive pulmonary disease (USDHHS, 1989). In 1990, approximately one of every five deaths (419,000) was attributed to tobacco use (CDC, 1993a). Even nonsmokers exposed to secondhand cigarette smoke suffer the adverse health effects of tobacco (EPA, 1992b).

There is a striking disparity in the incidence of tobacco-related disease and death rates between African American and white populations, particularly among males. Overall, the cancer mortality rate for blacks is 20% to 40% higher than that of the general population (National Cancer Institute, 1991). Death rates from specific cancer types reveal further disparities.

Between 1950 and 1990, lung cancer death rates have increased dramatically from 13.0 to 50.3 per 100,000; the rate of increase in lung cancer deaths is higher for black men than white men, however. While death rates from cancer of the larynx remained stable from 1950 to 1990 for whites, they increased 260% for black males and 233% for black females. The death rate from esophageal cancer is three times higher for black men, and the rate has doubled for black women while remaining stable for white women (CDC, 1993b). The disparity is true for other tobacco-related diseases as well. Despite the overall decline in coronary heart disease, the rate of decline is slower for African Americans (USDHHS, 1994a). In 1991, the coronary heart disease death rate was 156 per 100,000 for African Americans compared with 118 per 100,000 for the general population.

Despite general awareness of the dangers of tobacco, smoking remains widespread. Approximately 48 million adults smoked in 1994 (USDHHS, 1994b). Smoking prevalence has been higher in blacks than in whites since 1965 (National Center for Health Statistics, 1993b). Data from 1987 indicate that 34% of blacks smoked in 1987, compared with 29% of the general population. In 1992, the proportion of African Americans who smoked was still higher than that of the general population (USDHHS, 1994a). The higher rates reflect a difference in prevalence among men, whereas the rates for black and white women are comparable.

In addition to prevalence, the pattern of tobacco consumption differs between African Americans and whites (Robinson, Pertschuk, & Sutton, 1992). African Americans smoke fewer cigarettes per day (Robinson et al., 1992); the type of cigarettes smoked, however, can also affect health outcomes. A higher percentage of African American smokers (76% compared with 23% of white smokers in 1986) uses menthol cigarettes, which may contribute to higher cancer mortality rates, and more African American smokers (78%) than white smokers (56%) prefer cigarettes with high levels of tar (USDHHS, 1989). Similarly, 65% of African American smokers compared with 36% of white smokers use cigarettes with high nicotine content (greater than 1.1 mg), which contributes to addiction (USDHHS, 1988, 1989).

The mortality and morbidity caused by tobacco use are compounded by contextual factors affecting African American communities. For example, blacks are less likely to receive smoking cessation counseling from health care providers than are whites (34.4% vs. 38.2%; CDC, 1993c). In 1990, tobacco companies spent nearly $4 billion on cigarette advertising and promotion (USDHHS, 1994c). Consequently, the African American media have become dependent on tobacco advertising for their survival (Tuckson, 1989). Similarly, the tobacco industry has become a significant employer and chief supporter of cultural events, social services, political and civic organizations, education, and businesses in African American communities (Robinson et al., 1992). Thus, attempts to reduce tobacco may be hindered by the powerful presence of the tobacco industry in the community, the social norms that validate smoking, and the insufficient resources to counter contextual factors supporting unhealthy behavior.

Alcohol and Other Drugs

Like the use of tobacco, the use of illicit drugs and the misuse of alcohol create grave health and social problems. Alcohol contributes to chronic diseases including heart disease and hepatitis and is the principal cause of cirrhosis (Mosher, 1992; National Center for Health Statistics, 1993a). Alcohol is also a factor in approximately 50% of the deaths caused by motor vehicle crashes (Perrine, Peck, & Fell, 1989). Alcohol and other drugs (AOD) are implicated in a range of social ills including homelessness, homicide, suicide, and family violence (Gilliam, 1992; Prothrow-Stith & Weissman, 1991). In addition to the risk of death from overdose, intravenous drug use is a known transmission route of the human immunodeficiency virus that causes AIDS.

As with tobacco, AOD-related disease patterns indicate increased risks for African Americans. The following examples illustrate the health impact of substance abuse on African American communities. In 1991, cirrhosis death rates were 17.4 per 100,000 for black males and 8.3 for the nation (USDHHS, 1994a). Although African Americans constitute 12.3% of the U.S. population, 39% of the drug-related emergency room cases and 30% of the deaths were African Americans (National Institute on Drug Abuse, 1988). The rate of needle use is almost twice as high for African Americans as for whites (USDHHS,

TABLE 4.2 Prevalence of Cigarette, Alcohol, and Other Drug Use for African Americans and the General Population in 1994*

	African Americans (%)	General Population (%)
Cigarettes	30.6	31.7
Alcohol	55.8	66.9
Any illicit drug	12.5	10.8
Cocaine	2.9	1.7
Crack	1.6	0.6
Marijuana	10.2	8.5
Inhalant	0.5	1.1
Hallucinogen	1.3	0.5
Stimulant	0.5	0.7
Heroin	0.1	0.5

SOURCE: USDHHS (1994b).
* Estimate for "used past year."

1994b). In 1989, 44% of African Americans with AIDS reported intravenous drug injection prior to diagnosis, and more than 50% of the AIDS cases among heterosexual partners of intravenous drug users were African Americans. These patterns underscore the need to address AOD use to create healthy communities.

Overall, the prevalence of drug use has decreased among African Americans since 1988 (National Institute on Drug Abuse, 1990). Yet significant numbers of African Americans continue to use addictive drugs and alcohol. Table 4.2 indicates the comparison between the prevalence of drug users in African Americans and in the general population for selected substances. According to the 1994 *National Household Survey on Drug Abuse* (USDHHS, 1994b), the percentage of African Americans using alcohol in the previous year (55.8%) was less than that of the general population (66.9%). The percentages of African Americans using cocaine and marijuana were higher than those of the general population, and the rates of crack and hallucinogen use were more than twice those of the general population.

ATOD Prevention

Studies of effective prevention programs conclude that multiple strategies are required to affect ATOD use. Edwards (1990) reviewed several models for ATOD prevention and found that outstanding programs are comprehensive in scope; provide positive alternatives to unhealthy behaviors; develop life skills; educate significant people surrounding ATOD abusers (i.e., parents, teachers, and role models); and change social policy and community norms.

According to the surgeon general's report (USDHHS, 1994c), primary prevention activities for smoking should include increasing comprehensive school-based health education, reducing minors' access to tobacco products, more extensive counseling by health care providers about smoking cessation, developing and enacting strong clean indoor air policies and laws, restricting and eliminating advertising aimed at persons under 18 years of age, and increasing tobacco excise taxes. Similar strategies have been suggested for alcohol and drug use prevention, including raising the minimum drinking age, enforcing drinking and driving laws, prosecuting vendors selling to minors, and promoting positive images of abstinence in the media. As exemplified by the list above, strategies must address the socioecological setting of ATOD use and not just the behavior of the individual.

Simply knowing which prevention activities should be implemented is not sufficient. Chavis (1995) argues that a community must possess certain attributes and capacities that enable it to create successful prevention programs. To develop these capacities, he proposes that communities focus on the three principal areas of resource acquisition and mobilization, political capacities, and psychosocial attributes (Table 4.3).

The Afrocentric Perspective

In the past, many prevention efforts targeting African Americans have failed to take into account the cultural context of ATOD use. Consequently, the interventions have been inappropriate, and the results discouraging (Bouie, 1993). To correct this myopic prevention planning, Bouie calls for an Afrocentric perspective as the foundation for substance abuse programs. Bouie posits,

> Given the hostile environment in which they exist, it is critical to the survival and development of African Americans that we view alcohol and other drug abuse as a function of this experience in an oppressive environment. The Afrocentric perspective provides a guidepost for understanding alcohol and other drug abuse in the African American community, not in terms of the chemical, but in terms of the forces that initiate and perpetuate an individual's physical or psychological need to use that chemical.

Social injustice, social inconsistency, and the resulting personal impotence contribute to a sense of alienation that supports dysfunctional behavior including ATOD use. The roles of oppression, economic deprivation, racism, and other external stressors related to the African American experience must be acknowl-

TABLE 4.3 Areas of Capacity Building Required to Create a Learning Community

Resource Acquisition and Mobilization
- Increased resources for prevention and community development
- Recruitment and use of volunteers and other nonmonetary resources
- Fundraising strategies, structures, and resources
- Learning/intellectual attributes
- Knowledge and skills
- Enabling system (workshops, seminars, consultations, information and referral networks)

Political Capacities
- Interinstitutional linkages and practices that promote prevention and community development
- Setting goals and planning
- Goal attainment
- Process and structures that foster responsiveness and accountability
- Leadership development and support

Psychosocial Factors
- Mobilization and management of social relations
- Sense of community caring
- Development and maintenance of organizations and communities
- Appropriate and effective help seeking
- Organizational structure and climate

edged and dealt with in substance abuse prevention and control programs. Thus, the Afrocentric perspective commands that prevention efforts address the social ecology of substance abuse and not just the behavior of the addict.

THE USE OF COALITIONS IN ATOD PREVENTION

In a review of the attributes of successful prevention models, Edwards (1990) noted that collaboration is a key to successful programs. Evolving perspectives on prevention and encouraging results from health coalitions have led to the growing recognition of the value of partnerships in community-based substance abuse interventions. The result has been a proliferation of funding opportunities for local coalitions that address ATOD problems. This trend is documented by a 1993 survey that identified 2,200 groups nationwide that led or sponsored substance abuse coalitions (Join Together, 1993).

As noted in Chapter 2, the federal government and private foundations have put increased emphasis on coalition-building initiatives. One of the most significant supporters of ATOD coalitions is the Center for Substance Abuse Prevention, which, at its peak, awarded funding to 252 communities for coalition development (Kaftarian & Hansen, 1994). The Robert Wood Johnson Foundation has contributed to the growth of ATOD coalitions through its Fighting Back program, as has the National Institutes of Health through its support of the National Cancer Institute's COMMIT and ASSIST programs (Jellinek & Hearn, 1991; Thompson, Wallack, Lichtenstein, & Pechacek, 1990-1991).

The Role of the Coalition

A relatively clear understanding of the strategies required to decrease ATOD use has emerged from the literature. The unrelenting ATOD problem, however, is evidence of the difficulty of applying those strategies and bringing about change. Hailed as state of the art in ATOD prevention, coalitions seem a promising solution, but there is still some uncertainty about how coalitions can best be used to implement the required strategies.

Reviews of the literature (Butterfoss et al., 1993; Chavis, 1995; Chavis, Speer, Resnick, & Zippay, 1993) have identified the following primary functions of community-based prevention coalitions:

- Broaden the mission of member organizations and develop more comprehensive strategies

- Develop wider public support for issues

- Increase the influence of individual community institutions over community policies and practices

- Minimize duplication of services

- Develop more financial and human resources

- Increase participation from diverse sectors and constituencies

- Exploit new resources in a changing environment

- Increase accountability

- Improve capacity to plan and evaluate

- Strengthen local organizations and institutions to respond better to the needs and aspirations of their constituents

This list suggests that a coalition's most important function is to increase the capacity of the community at large and of the member organizations to implement prevention activities. This view is consistent with Chavis's (1995) concept of the *learning community,* which he describes as a community in which organizations and individuals have the capacity to continually learn and expand together toward a collective vision. He argues that the purpose of a coalition is to promote the development of a learning community by facilitating the growth of the capacities listed above. These tools or capacities are developed through the fortification of grassroots organizations (Chavis, Florin, & Felix, 1993). Coalitions can support the growth of grassroots organizations by providing resources, incentives, and education.

The Role of Empowerment

An important attribute of coalitions is their ability to empower individuals and member organizations. Member organizations of coalitions benefit by increased local ownership of projects, and communities are empowered through the experience of effecting positive change. In short, the work of the coalition can be empowering to the individuals, the member organizations, and the community in which the coalition is embedded. Although Chavis (1995) did not explicitly so state, it seems evident that empowerment, the process of gaining and exerting control over important issues in one's life, is an attribute of a learning community and therefore should be considered one of the essential functions of a coalition.

To explore how the concept of empowerment applies to coalitions, McMillan, Florin, Stevenson, Kerman, and Mitchell (1995) studied 35 ATOD coalitions. They found that members' participation and the organizational climate of the coalition are the most significant contributors to the psychological empowerment of individuals in a coalition. Assessment of participation is based on the number of hours per month spent on various coalition activities, participation roles, and the benefits and the costs of participation. Organizational climate is related to such attributes as the degree of involvement of members, the organization and focus of tasks, member satisfaction with coalition experience, and the level of commitment to the coalition. McMillan et al. found organizational climate, benefits to the group, a collective level of commitment, and a strong sense of community to be the most important characteristics that are empowering to the coalition (as opposed to the individual members).

The question of what characteristics of a coalition are associated with being organizationally empowered is also instructive. An organizationally empowered coalition is one that can achieve its objectives and alter the contextual factors contributing to ATOD use. McMillan et al. (1995) found that organizational climate was key; organizations that were more focused, inclusive, and satisfactory to members had the greatest impact.

Fawcett et al. (1995) explored what model of community empowerment is best suited to enhance community capacity. They concluded that coalitions should act as enabling organizations that empower member organizations to influence conditions affecting health and development. In other words, the empowerment of local organizations is a prerequisite to changing health outcomes in the community. Coalitions or collaborative partnerships can enable the empowerment process by providing technical assistance and support.

Braithwaite and Lythcott (1989) proposed a community organization and development model as an antecedent to community empowerment. This model was applied to 35 communities in rural Georgia to address substance abuse (Braithwaite, 1994). Using the model, the community gains control over health promotion activities through the development of a coalition of health and human service providers and health care consumers. The coalition then becomes responsible for conducting a community needs assessment, implementing interventions, and conducting evaluations. Through training, there is a transfer of knowledge and social science technology from researchers to coalition members, which results in increased community capacity for ATOD prevention and the initiation of the empowerment process.

In short, the process of coalition development can trigger community empowerment. Coalitions have the potential to empower individuals, member organizations, and the community and to facilitate capacity building so that the community has the skills to tackle ATOD use.

Contextual Factors Affecting Coalitions

Coalitions do not operate in a vacuum. Their functioning is affected by many factors in the community context in which ATOD use occurs. Wandersman et al. (1996) reviewed the national evaluations of the formative phases of the Center for Substance Abuse Prevention's Community Demonstration Project and the Robert Wood Johnson Foundation's Fighting Back Initiative. They found four contextual factors critical to coalition formation and maintenance: (1) demographic characteristics, (2) economic conditions, (3) politics and religion, and (4) the presence of related prevention activities independent of the partnership.

Demographic Context

Several obstacles related to the diversity within the community were encountered (Wandersman et al., 1996). By definition, coalitions should be inclusive, bringing together diverse interest groups. In some cases, coalition formation marked the first time that ethnic groups in historically divided communities had come together to solve common problems (Stewart & Klitzner, 1993). In others, however, the racial and ethnic diversity resulted in distrust and competition between coalition members.

Many factors can hinder or encourage inclusion and participation of diverse groups. Cultural and language barriers may limit participation. At times, key ethnic groups will not be included, giving rise to tension within the coalition and a lack of acceptance of the coalition by the community. Another problem is related to the strategy of creating a coalition that is representative of the ethnic and racial composition of the community. If the coalition simply invites a few individuals from key organizations to speak for the interests of an entire ethnic group, the coalition will fail to represent the diversity within any ethnic group. Perceptions of inclusion particularly may be a problem if the lead agency is an external organization of predominantly white, middle-class, and professional members (Stewart & Klitzner, 1993).

Similarly, Wandersman et al. (1996) found that differences in social class can pose a challenge to coalitions. They cited one example of a coalition in which disagreements arose between the middle-class and poor African Americans about control over the planning process. In another case, poor Hispanics did not feel that their interests were represented by Hispanics from more established communities.

In their evaluation of the Robert Wood Johnson Foundation's Fighting Back Initiative, Stewart and Klitzner (1993) identified social class as a barrier to coalition development. For example, some coalitions dominated by middle-class citizens focused their prevention efforts on low-income, inner-city residents; coalition members representing disadvantaged groups, however, felt this focus was inappropriate because drug use and arrests frequently involve middle-class, suburban residents. These examples demonstrate that even in a community of racial or ethnic homogeneity, the importance of social class cannot be dismissed.

Age distribution in the community can also affect coalition formation. Wandersman et al. (1996) found 15 sites in which the communities were predominantly young and poor. The power elites, however, tended to be older residents from the middle class. Disparate perceptions between the two groups about community needs and priorities led to disagreements about the goals of the coalition.

Economic Context

The economic context includes developments in both the national and local economy. Anticipated developments may also affect the functioning of the coalition. Examples include downsizing and job insecurity in the military or high-tech sectors and declines in manufacturing.

Political and Religious Context

In the Robert Wood Johnson Foundation's Fighting Back coalitions, political and religious factors posed a significant challenge. Whether the coalition's goals were consistent with the local government's concerns was key. If there are competing concerns, the government may be limited in the time and resources it can commit to the coalition. Stewart and Klitzner (1993) found that communities with city manager-led governments or weak mayors were more willing to make unpopular decisions or go against strong interest groups (i.e., tobacco industry and business) to make changes in the social environment. Such decisions are essential for ATOD prevention.

Considering the religious orientation of a community is important to coalition formation. Religious leaders are often trusted members of the community who can improve the credibility of a coalition. Incorporating representatives from the faith community into the coalition leadership has enabled coalitions to increase grassroots participation (Stewart & Klitzner, 1993).

Prevention Context

The final contextual factor reported by Wandersman et al. (1996) is the existence of other prevention activities in the community. Other activities may support or compete with the coalition goals. One should assess the coexisting initiatives to avoid competition and duplication of effort.

EVALUATING ATOD COALITIONS

The evaluation of coalitions is still a relatively new phenomenon. The use of coalitions appeals to common sense and current health promotion attitudes that place a high value on community involvement in decision making and problem solving. Although at this time, little evidence supports the assumption that coalitions are uniquely able to develop new programs and reduce the impact of ATOD use (Chavis, 1995; Gerstein & Green, 1993), many advances in evaluation methodology are being applied to coalitions and will lead to a better understanding of this important strategy (Kaftarian & Hansen, 1994).

Much has been written in recent years in response to the need for more information on the value of ATOD coalitions. What factors promote coalition building? What factors affect participation levels? What factors influence the acceptance of prevention programs by the community? What has been the impact of the prevention programs developed by the coalition? All these questions are important to the functioning and effectiveness of a coalition, and they can be addressed with formative, process, and summative evaluation.

Evaluation of ATOD coalitions poses many challenges, including the difficulty of imposing a quasi-experimental evaluation design in a community setting; measuring the effects of multiple, simultaneous interventions; and the long time lapse between the initiation and termination of many interventions (Kim, Crutchfield, Williams, & Hepler, 1994). Researchers studying models of coalition building that promote community ownership struggle to preserve scientific integrity in their evaluation research (Thompson et al., 1990-1991). In response, program evaluators are developing innovative evaluation methods and designs to provide the much needed information. The following section reviews some of the evaluation innovations for single- and multiple-site programs that substance abuse coalitions may find instructive. Table 4.4 summarizes the evaluation questions and methods associated with each phase of coalition development and maintenance.

Formative Evaluation

Formative evaluation is a planning tool. It is conducted to ensure that coalition formation is proceeding as planned and that the coalition develops the attributes that contribute to effective community action. It corresponds to the first phase in the life of a coalition, mobilization and formation. A formative evaluation seeks to answer questions about member recruitment, participation, and satisfaction and the establishment of a coalition's mandate, objectives, plan, and organizational structure. If problems are found during formative evaluation, coalition members can make adjustments so that the outcome of the coalition's work is not jeopardized.

Goodman, Wandersman, Chinman, Imm, and Morrissey (1996) use a variety of evaluation tools to monitor the formation of a coalition in their work with the Midlands Prevention Alliance, a partnership of 22 substance abuse, HIV and STD, and violence coalitions in South Carolina. They have created the *forecast* evaluation, described in detail in Goodman and Wandersman (1994). In the forecast evaluation design, evaluators work with the coalition members to create a model or diagram of the problems to be addressed by the partnership, identify markers that indicate the progress toward the goal, develop measures to determine if a marker has been attained, and interpret the meaning of the development indicators. Measures are based on program documentation such as meeting minutes and staff activity calendars (Goodman et al., 1996). To provide more precise information on the effectiveness of the coalition's meetings, the evaluators have created a Meeting Effectiveness Inventory that asks participants to rank the meeting in the areas of leadership, participation, decision making, conflict resolution, and productivity. These data are supplemented with a Project Insight Form in which an open-ended interview schedule

TABLE 4.4 Summary of Evaluation Types, Indicators, and Data Collection Methods
           for ATOD Coalitions

Evaluation Type	Indicators	Data Collection Methods
Formative evaluation: concerned with aspects of coalition formation	• Number and composition of membership • Quality of leadership • Participation levels • Member satisfaction • Creation of governing structure • Definition of coalition's mandate and objectives • Development of prevention plans	• Meeting Effectiveness Inventory/ Surveys on committee functioning[a,c] • Project Insight Form completed by meeting chair[a] • Meeting minutes[a] • Staff Activity calendars[a] • Community Needs Assessment Checklist • Plan Quality Index[a] • Ethnography of drug use culture[d]
Process evaluation: concerned with the implementation of project plans	• Correlation between activities and plans • Pattern of formation • Membership composition • Functions of the coalition • Stage of organizational development	• Written questionnaires on coalition functioning[b] • Meeting minutes[b] • Tracking of action logs[a] • Ethnography of the culture of the partnership[d]

Summative evaluation: concerned with the impact of the interventions on the ATOD use and health outcomes and the sustainability of the coalition's programs	• Changes in knowledge, attitudes, or behavior related to ATOD use in the community
	• Changes in the contextual factors including changes in policy and legislation
	• Social and health indicators:
	  - ATOD mortality and morbidity
	  - Tobacco and alcohol sales
	  - Enrollment in drug and alcohol rehabilitation and smoking cessation programs
	  - Participation in needle exchange programs
	  - Illicit drug arrests
	  - Blood alcohol levels in car wreck fatalities
		• Interviews with key leaders[a]
		• Survey of community members
		• Existing data systems:[a]
		  - Health care facilities
		  - Human service agencies
		  - Criminal justice systems
		• Ethnography of changes in social norms related to ATOD use[d]

[a]Goodman et al. (1996); [b]Mansergh et al. (1996); [c]Butterfoss, Goodman, Wandersman, Valois, & Chinman (1996); [d]Hunt (1994).

is administered to the meeting chairperson. All results are shared with the coalition members.

Another method employed in formative evaluation is a survey and feedback process (Butterfoss, Goodman, Wandersman, Valois, & Chinman, 1996). Coalition members complete a written questionnaire that elicits information on the functioning of the committees within the coalition. The questionnaire covers aspects of committee climate, leadership, task orientation, costs, and benefits of participation. Results can be aggregated and used to create committee profiles, which are included in a handbook along with strategies to improve problem areas. Using this method, Butterfoss, Goodman, and Wandersman (1996) found that member satisfaction is a key indicator in a formative evaluation because it is an important factor in the success of mobilization, the development of organizational structure, and capacity building. Thus, member satisfaction is critical to the maintenance of a coalition through time. They also found that conditions that lead to member satisfaction and participation include competent leadership, influence in decision making, the number of linkages with other organizations, and a supportive environment that facilitates task orientation.

Formative evaluation is also concerned with the creation of community plans that occurs after members are mobilized. The community plan usually grows from the needs, resources, and priorities identified in a community analysis. Evaluators for the Midlands Prevention Alliance (Goodman et al., 1996) have developed a Needs Assessment Checklist to monitor the coalition's community analysis and a Plan Quality Index to measure the quality of its plan. These tools are discussed elsewhere (Butterfoss, Goodman, & Wandersman, 1996; Butterfoss, Goodman, Wandersman, Valois, et al., 1996). Butterfoss, Goodman, and Wandersman (1996) did not find that a high degree of member satisfaction necessarily resulted in the development of good community plans. Similarly, Stewart and Klitzner (1993) point out that the simple existence of collectivity does not ensure the development of a viable or effective community plan. Plans developed by a coalition may be consensual, but they frequently lag behind the current knowledge of substance abuse prevention.

Ethnography is another tool that is beginning to receive the attention of program evaluators who deal with substance abuse. Traditional survey methods are often unable to collect information on drug culture and hard-to-reach populations such as drug users and dealers (Hunt, 1994). Ethnography, the "systematic description of a culture based on firsthand participation" (Braithwaite, Bianchi, & Taylor, 1994, p. 409), offers an alternative method of data collection. Participant observation, an activity in which the researcher records his or her observations while participating in daily cultural events, is the conventional tool of the ethnographer. Braithwaite et al. propose the use of ethnographic techniques to document the needs of a community, which is the first step to community planning. Ethnography is particularly suitable for revealing the cultural characteristics that influence ATOD use.

Process evaluation

The second phase of coalition development is implementation or the translation of the project plans into action. The long-term impact of a coalition's prevention program will depend in part on the functioning of the coalition and on how well the coalition's plans are implemented. Process-level indicators are required to measure this aspect of a partnership. Process evaluation allows evaluators to determine the utility of coalition models and how well members are adhering to the model.

Mansergh, Rohrach, Montgomery, Pentz, and Johnson (1996) suggest several indicators based on the literature to measure the immediate process and activity outcomes that negotiate the transition from coalition formation to achievement of the desired health impact. Process-level indicators include the pattern of formation, the membership composition, the organizational structure, the functions of the coalition, and the stage of organizational development.

A variety of methods have been employed to measure process indicators. Mansergh et al. (1996) used written questionnaires consisting of Likert scale questions to survey coalition members about their perceptions of coalition functioning. They also reviewed meeting minutes and other documents to examine the achievements of action committees.

Goodman et al. (1996) offer another strategy for process evaluation based on a method proposed by Francisco, Paine, and Fawcett (1993). "Tracking of Action" logs are kept to follow the progress of project implementation. On the logs, coalition staff record information on various aspects of implementation, and the data are compiled monthly to mark the immediate outcomes and cumulatively to indicate trends through time. Hunt (1994) advocates the use of ethnography in process evaluation. Using this method, an evaluator can examine the "culture of the partnership" to gauge the development and functioning of the coalition.

Summative Evaluation

This last type of evaluation looks at the impacts of a health intervention. A coalition's prevention projects should result in increased awareness, changes in the contextual factors that support ATOD use, and, ultimately, in a reduction of substance use. In addition to the impact of the coalition's efforts on the community, summative evaluations may consider the likelihood that the coalition's work will be sustained after the initial funding. This transition occurs with the institutionalization of the coalition's activities. Summative evaluation corresponds to the maintenance and outcome stage of coalition development.

Goodman et al. (1996) interviewed the heads of service organizations as one gauge of the coalition's impact in the Midlands Prevention Alliance. The rationale for using these key leaders to measure community-level changes is based on the premise that they are sentinels that signal changes in the community. Furthermore, positively influencing key leaders' attitudes and beliefs is likely to result in greater support for ATOD prevention programs and policies.

Surveying community residents is an alternative method for assessing the impact of the coalition on community residents. For example, the Center for Substance Abuse Prevention's Community Partnership Demonstration Program has developed a survey to collect data on ATOD beliefs, attitudes, and use from adults in the target population. Other estimates of impact can be obtained from data on health outcomes or risk behavior from existing data systems in health care facilities, human service agencies, or criminal justice systems (Goodman et al., 1996). Indicators can include enrollment in drug rehabilitation programs, participation in needle exchange programs, illegal drug arrests, and blood alcohol levels of car wreck fatalities. These data, which indicate the changes in community health, ATOD availability, and policy changes, can be compared with the timing of the coalition's activities to indicate association.

Ethnography can also be used as a summative evaluation tool (Hunt, 1994). With this qualitative method, the evaluator can explore "ATOD use culture" to identify normative changes through time resulting from an intervention.

ATOD COALITION AND PARTNERSHIP EXAMPLES

The following examples of ATOD coalitions and partnerships reported in the literature should give the reader an indication of the range of possibilities.

The Uptown Coalition

The Uptown Coalition in Philadelphia made history as the first African American coalition to successfully fight the tobacco industry. Even more impressive is that this community-based coalition evolved without any financial support from the major agencies that fund such initiatives. The Uptown Coalition is a testament to the power of the coalition as a tool in the fight to save communities from the devastating effects of tobacco (Robinson et al., 1992).

The coalition formed in direct response to the efforts of the R. J. Reynolds Tobacco Company to market a cigarette that specifically targeted African American communities. In addition to the victory over the tobacco company, the coalition's efforts had several important outcomes. It offered a model of successful community mobilization and empowerment. It led to new ways of thinking about and defining tobacco issues that took the focus away from individuals and placed it on the behavior of the tobacco industry. It promoted media advocacy as a means of countering the industry's traditional use of the media to influence social norms. Finally, it helped to forge a relationship between African American leaders and tobacco control advocacy organizations that are historically white-dominated organizations.

Community Intervention Trial for Smoking Cessation

The National Cancer Institute has undertaken a research project to study the effectiveness of a community-based approach to smoking cessation. Although many smoking cessation programs focus on changing the behavior of the smoker, a conventional health promotion approach, the Community Intervention Trial for Smoking Cessation (COMMIT; Thompson et al., 1990-1991) seeks to influence the broader sociopolitical context in which tobacco use takes place.

Its commitment to modifying the environment around smoking is exemplified by COMMIT's goals to (a) increase the priority of smoking as a public health issue, (b) increase the community capacity to modify smoking behavior, (c) increase the influence of existing policy and economic factors within a community that discourage smoking, and (d) increase social norms and values supporting nonsmoking. To achieve these goals, COMMIT advocates the formation of a partnership between outside professionals, including health educators and researchers, and community members. The partnership approach is based on the principle of true collaboration in which each partner participates in decision making. The partnership builds on existing community structures and seeks to enhance their capacity to reduce smoking, rather than create new structures that compete for resources and are unlikely to be sustained after the funding period.

COMMIT has developed a model of community mobilization and partnership formation that creates a standardized approach to prevention across diverse sites but is flexible enough to allow each community partnership to develop according to its unique circumstances. The first step to mobilization is to conduct an intensive community analysis that examines the possible intervention opportunities and the characteristics of the community that may facilitate or inhibit the partnership's success. Ten of the communities involved in the COMMIT project were located throughout the United States, and one was located in Ontario, Canada. Their settings and sizes ranged from small towns (population of 59,000) to urban centers (population of 163,000), and ethnic minorities constituted 3.7% to 58.9% of the population of the communities. Communities also varied in the percentage of smokers. The most common facilitating factors identified by the community analyses were a cooperative environment for community improvement, a supportive health care environment, a history of volunteerism, and active citizen participation in community leadership. The inhibiting factors included community tension, economic problems, and difficulty with the media.

From the community analysis, the key sectors required to address the problem were identified, and individuals from these sectors were recruited to form a community planning group. The community planning group is a temporary assembly of knowledgeable citizens whose purpose is to assist in the development of the permanent community board. The community board structure has a minimum of four task forces: public education, health care, work site and organizations, and cessation resources and services. Once established, the community boards are responsible for partnership development (e.g., define mandate, develop bylaws, and recruit members) and for creating management plans for project implementation.

Ujima

Bouie (1993) describes the *Ujima* approach based on an Afrocentric perspective of ATOD use. *Ujima,* meaning collective work and responsibility, symbolizes the cultural underpinnings of this approach, which uses a community organization and mobilization model to form a partnership or core group. Bouie lists the following as essential members of the core group in an African American community: schools, the criminal justice system, street workers, public housing, community leaders, African American-owned media, and community communication systems. The core group partnership provides a leadership structure for setting community action goals and implementing strategies to meet them.

Community Partnership Demonstration Program

As noted previously, the Center for Substance Abuse Prevention has been one of the leading agencies to support coalition building as a strategy to reduce alcohol and drug use in communities. Since 1990, the Center for Substance Abuse Prevention has sponsored the Community Partnership Demonstration Program, a comprehensive community-based program that is designed to bring together key public and private organizations (Kaftarian & Hansen, 1994). The community coalitions either facilitate and coordinate existing prevention activities to reduce duplication and encourage appropriate distribution of resources or create prevention programs where needs are not being met. In 1993, the program's most active period, 252 communities received funding. Throughout

TABLE 4.5 Organizations Most Frequently Belonging to Center for Substance Abuse
Prevention-Funded AOD Coalitions

Type of Organization	Most Common Membership Category (Percentage)
Volunteer groups	6.9
Churches	6.1
Alcohol and other drug abuse programs	5.6
Schools	5.6
Business organizations	5.2

NOTE: $N = 962$.

the program, the Center for Substance Abuse Prevention has encouraged evaluation of program sites.

Using data collected on process evaluation forms from program sites, we can
provide a description of coalitions serving communities with African American
populations. Of the 252 coalitions funded in 1993, 18 were in communities in
which African Americans composed 40% or more of the total population. Only
these 18 coalitions will be included in this discussion. The site locations ranged
from the Virgin Islands to Los Angeles in predominantly large jurisdictions
(population more than 250,000). The membership of the coalitions ranged from
9 to 112 organizations. The most common member organizations were (a) volunteer organizations, (b) churches, (c) alcohol and other drug abuse programs,
(d) schools, and (e) business organizations (see Table 4.5).

Some of the organizations least frequently represented in the coalitions
included parent groups, parent-teacher associations, public health clinics, private mental health organizations, and welfare and public assistance agencies.
The most common reason cited by members for withdrawing from the coalition
was lack of time (38%). Other reasons included change of coalition leadership
and representatives changing positions.

All the coalitions had established a board as a governing structure; the degree
of functioning of the board varied, however, and was likely to affect the
productivity of the coalition. Thirteen (72%) had developed bylaws. The most
frequently listed functions of the steering committee were to plan (89%) and to
set policies (83%). Other functions included coordination (72%) and budget
review (56%). Fourteen coalitions reported either having completed or being in
the process of developing an AOD plan. Of these, 12 were city- or countywide
plans. Most plans specified collaborating partners (79%) and suggested specific
programs (86%). Fewer (64%) had outlined specific goals for the coalition, and
only one had provided for a prevention coordinator.

Coalitions coordinated many existing AOD interventions and created them
if none existed. The most common AOD activities reported by the 18 coalitions

TABLE 4.6 Most Frequent AOD Prevention Activities Facilitated or Created by Center for Substance Abuse Prevention-Funded Coalitions

Activity	Number*
Community forums	15
Technical assistance	14
Alternative activities for youth	13
Media campaign	13
School-based prevention	12
Cultural or ethnic festivals and events	11
Team building	11
Community advocacy	10
Training	10
Community development	9
Mentoring programs	9
Parent education	9

NOTE: * The number of activities facilitated or created by 18 coalitions; a total of 200 activities were facilitated or created by the coalitions.

focused predominantly on modifying contextual factors in the community (e.g., media campaigns, alternative activities for youth, and cultural events) and building community capacity (e.g., technical assistance, training, team building, and community development). (See Table 4.6.) In contrast, fewer activities provided substance abuse treatment (1); individual, family, or group counseling services (5); or other programs promoting behavior change for substance users. These activities are consistent with the recommended functions of a coalition described in the literature. A coalition's primary function is not to provide service delivery but to increase the community's and the member organizations' capacity to plan and implement prevention activities and to gain wider public support for prevention (Butterfoss et al., 1993; Chavis, 1995; Chavis, Florin, & Felix, 1993).

An indication of the outcomes of the coalitions' efforts is given by the products produced for prevention activities. Newsletters were the most frequent product produced (29), followed by press releases (25), brochures (25), and training materials (21). Other products included videos, directories of prevention services, and posters.

These data address formative and process evaluation questions. They indicate to what extent coalitions were able to solidify into functioning collaborative partnerships based on the mobilization of member organizations, formation of a governing board, development of bylaws, functions of the steering committee, and the development and quality of community prevention plans. The data suggest that coalitions succeeded in forming viable governing structures and systems but had greater difficulty creating detailed prevention plans and objectives. Coalitions were able to facilitate or create a variety of prevention activities that primarily addressed capacity building and modification of the context in which AOD use takes place and produced educational products. The prevalence and incidence of AOD use must be examined to determine the long-term health impact of the coalitions.

Coalitions have received much attention in recent years as a strategy for reducing and preventing ATOD use in African American communities. As the Center for Substance Abuse Prevention example illustrates, coalitions are capable of launching a multipronged, comprehensive prevention and control intervention to modify the environmental factors influencing ATOD use, build the community's capacity to implement prevention activities once funding has ended, and facilitate individual behavior change if necessary. Such a multifaceted approach is necessary to combat the complex issues surrounding ATOD use. Continuing evaluation is required to determine the long-term ability of coalitions to affect ATOD use; advances in evaluation methodology, however, have yielded instruments and evaluation designs to facilitate the application of this important tool in the fight against debilitating effects of ATOD use in communities.

5

The Black Faith Community and Public Health

The black faith community and public health providers have worked together for many years to improve the health of African Americans in the United States. Blacks suffer disproportionately compared with whites from heart disease, strokes, cancer, and many other illnesses (Braithwaite & Taylor, 1992). This disparity has been a prime factor motivating the alliance between black clergy and health professionals to improve the health of black Americans. The historic role and mission of the black church have made it a powerful institution for serving the health needs of the black community.

This chapter provides information and examples for those considering collaboration with the black faith community on health interventions. The benefits of working together on health problems both to black religious institutions and to health professionals and service agencies are outlined early in the chapter. The key role of church volunteers, or lay health advisers, in these interventions is described, followed by a discussion of the selection and training of the lay health advisers. Examples of projects aimed at combating various health problems are presented. Finally, limitations found by health providers collaborating with black churches are noted. The chapter begins by considering the connection between the mission of black religious institutions and the promotion of health among African Americans.

THE BLACK FAITH COMMUNITY AND HEALTH

Any discussion of cooperation among African Americans must naturally begin with a discussion of the black church. The church is the oldest institution in black America. It is one of the few institutions that is black controlled and designed to meet the needs of African Americans (Williams & Williams, 1984). In addition to being a place of worship, the black church has played a key role in the social and political activities of the black community. From it originated many slave insurrections and the inspiration, leadership, and resources for the civil rights movement (Du Bois, 1907; Haines, 1988; Morris, 1984). From the black church grew mutual aid societies that assisted economically in times of illness and with burial expenses and that served as forerunners of black entrepreneurial enterprises (Frazier, 1963; Williams & Williams, 1984). Black followers of the Islamic faith have also made a significant contribution to the struggle for civil rights. They are recognized for founding schools and businesses, developing crime prevention and security programs in poor neighborhoods, and working with persons who are incarcerated (Battle, 1988; Haines, 1988; McCloud, 1995). Attention to both the material and spiritual aspects of health and healing has always been a part of African American worship. Involvement in public health projects that improve the health of African Americans is a natural extension of the black religious community's service to the black community.

Research has been conducted to determine what type of black church is most likely to become involved in outreach programs. Lincoln and Mamiya (1990) report that urban black churches cooperate much more than rural churches with social agencies and non-church programs in dealing with community problems. They also note that black churches were more likely to work with civil rights organizations than with any other type of organization. A study of the characteristics of northern black churches that participate in community health outreach programs found that a positive association between church size and the educational level of the minister was the strongest predictor of church-sponsored community outreach programs (Thomas, Quinn, Billingsley, & Caldwell, 1994). Thomas et al.'s study suggests that the availability of paid clergy and other paid staff to provide consistent leadership to various programs is a necessary factor that determines the extent to which the church can continue the provision of community health outreach programs.

Another study, conducted in poor urban areas in the South Side of Chicago, sought to determine the interest of churches in sponsoring maternal and child health programs (Olson, Reis, Murphy, & Gehm, 1988). Church representatives did not see health problems as a high priority compared with such problems as unemployment, teenage pregnancy, and gang crime. In general, however, health professionals have found that most black churches are receptive when approached with a proposal to start a collaborative public health project.

In addition to taking an active role in collaborative health interventions with public health workers, the black faith community has taken the lead as the voice for African Americans on health issues. The Nation of Islam has spoken out about the shortage of physicians in inner-city and rural areas. It has pointed out through its minister of health that even universal insurance will not guarantee health coverage for all where access is a problem (Ellison, 1994). The First Baptist Institutional Church in Detroit worked with Blue Cross/Blue Shield to provide health care for children whose parents made too much money to be eligible for Medicaid but could not afford private insurance ("Churches, Blues," 1994). Black clergy have headed the campaign against the targeting of African Americans by tobacco companies. They led the struggle against the production of Uptown cigarettes by marketers and the fight opposing billboard advertising of tobacco products in black neighborhoods (McCollum, 1994). Dr. Deborah Prothrow-Stith, a United Methodist layperson and associate dean of Harvard University's school of public health, has promoted with the United Methodist Church the identification of violence as a public health problem and has pointed out its disproportionate effect on young black men ("Tackling Youth Violence," 1992).

Health awareness in the black Seventh-Day Adventist Church can be traced for more than 100 years, when church leaders emphasized the body as the temple of the Holy Spirit. In the mid-1800s, Ellen White, a key leader of the Seventh-Day Adventist Church, placed emphasis on providing health care services to freed slaves in the South. Since the 1830s, the Seventh-Day Adventist Church has adopted health reform, encouraging a diet free of pork products and other unclean animals and a lifestyle that excludes the use of alcohol and tobacco. Black Seventh-Day Adventists opened their own health sanitariums in the early 1900s in Nashville and Washington, D.C., with emphasis on natural healing and primary care. Presently, black Seventh-Day Adventist researchers are looking at health benefits to blacks who are actively involved in the church in Atlanta, Georgia; Alameda County, California; and other communities (Rock, 1996).

Larger churches and religious coalitions have the resources to develop and sustain large programs with their own funds and outside grants. The Concord Baptist Church in Brooklyn, perhaps the largest black church in New York City, owns an entire block of social service institutions; among these is a community health care center that the church runs with St. Mary's Hospital. Another example in Brooklyn is the House of the Lord, which led a 42-church coalition that received a $1.4 million grant from the city to house and support persons with AIDS. In Harlem, 50 churches and two mosques that joined together to develop an AIDS program were also awarded a $1.4 million grant (Rubin, Billingsley, & Caldwell, 1994). Although this chapter focuses on collaborative projects among the black faith community and public health professionals, black churches and mosques also serve as the voice for the black community with regard to a multitude of social health issues.

THE BENEFITS OF COLLABORATION
WITH BLACK RELIGIOUS INSTITUTIONS

Public health officials have realized that there are many benefits to collaborating with churches in solving public health problems. Churches have sponsored programs to deal with problems such as hypertension, obesity, diabetes, and high cholesterol. Programs can be readily generalized on a national level because religious institutions exist in every community (Lasater, Wells, Carleton, & Elder, 1986). One of the greatest advantages of working with churches is that the sustained social support they provide can be effective in initiating and maintaining health-promoting behavioral change among members of their congregations (Lasater et al., 1986; Olson et al., 1988). Public health professionals can use the overlapping networks among friends, families, church leaders, members of church groups, and church congregations to improve the health behavior of individuals (Eng & Hatch, 1991). Eng, Hatch, and Callan (1985) argue that the efficacy of an institution in promoting behavioral change is related to the degree to which the members of that institution feel connected with each other and share a common identity and purpose. They believe that because of this principle, black churches are especially powerful institutions for promoting positive behavioral change. This sense of group identity in rural areas is so strong among African Americans that their communities are frequently identified by the name of the church that serves them (Eng et al., 1985; Hatch & Lovelace, 1980). The frequent contact between congregation members and professional and volunteer health workers in church-based programs encourages adherence to prescribed therapeutic regimens (Kong, Miller, & Smoot, 1982).

Public health workers have found that collaborating with black churches is an effective form of outreach. Churches are better able to disseminate information within the wider black community than are other local organizations because of their relatively large memberships (DePue, Wells, Lasater, & Carleton, 1987; Lasater et al., 1986). Religious institutions have an impact not only on members of their congregations but also on the members' families (Lasater et al., 1986). While establishing black churches as high blood pressure control centers, Kong et al. (1982) found that churches can influence hard-to-reach populations through family members. Female family members, who are more likely to attend church, can encourage hard-to-reach young black men to become concerned about their blood pressure. The women may also share physiological and dietary knowledge with the men.

Religious institutions have resources that can be pooled with those of public health agencies to develop and sustain programs. Most places of worship have adequate space and meeting rooms to sponsor public health projects (Johnson, 1980; Lasater et al., 1986). Sometimes, religious organizations are able to allocate funds toward the health projects that they sponsor. This is especially helpful in difficult fiscal times when public resources are reduced (Johnson, Grossman, & Cassidy, 1996; Olson et al., 1988). Churches also efficiently provide volunteer labor. Volunteering is institutionalized in the black church because of its long history of community service (Johnson, 1980; Lasater et al., 1986; Olson et al., 1988).

Sponsorship by black churches provides legitimacy to programs initiated by social welfare agencies (Johnson, 1980). Distrust of health professionals and official agencies may limit the outreach of public health organizations that do not collaborate with a trusted community institution (Olson et al., 1988). This is especially true in African American communities in which a significant proportion of the population fears that public health agencies conspire to commit genocide against blacks (Thomas & Quinn, 1993). Some level of distrust of public health institutions by blacks is understandable given their mistreatment at the hands of the U.S. Public Health Service in the Tuskegee experiment (Jones, 1993; Thomas & Quinn, 1993). In 1987, a Black Coalition Caucus was formed by individuals involved in AIDS issues (Thomas & Quinn, 1993). It turned to the black clergy and churches to assure them that CDC programs in the black community were not repeating the mistakes of the Tuskegee experiment. Allaying fears of members of the black community about public health interventions may be one of the greatest benefits for public health professionals of collaborating with religious institutions. The Nation of Islam's minister of health has pointed out that a long-term solution to reducing the distrust of the medical establishment by minorities is to increase the number of minority health workers (Ellison, 1994).

THE ROLE OF LAY HEALTH ADVISERS

Public health interventions that result from collaboration between health professionals and the black faith community rely on volunteer health workers from the congregations. These men and women are neither health professionals nor clergy members but are trained in the basic health skills and knowledge necessary to assist other church members with health problems related to the aims of the particular project. For example, a lay health adviser or lay health leader helping with a hypertension project would be taught about the physiology of hypertension, how to properly measure blood pressure, behavioral aspects of blood pressure control, and how to connect at-risk individuals with medical professionals. The main criterion by which lay health advisers are selected from the congregation is that they are people to whom others naturally turn for advice and support. Therefore, they can motivate positive change in the health-related behaviors of their fellow parishioners (Eng & Hatch, 1991). These volunteers, along with the clergy, are the liaisons between the health professionals and the church members.

A key concept in the Seventh-Day Adventist church is that of the health and temperance leader. Lay health advisers are primarily responsible for health outreach and health promotion and establish health intervention programs for community and church members. These leaders link with health care providers to address major health concerns of the community (Rock, 1996).

The lay health advisers play many important roles in collaborative health projects. Perhaps the most important of those roles is as a catalyst for individual behavioral change. As individuals already deeply embedded in the natural support structures of the black church, the lay health advisers are able to help motivate and sustain through mutual support networks healthier lifestyles among fellow church members (Eng et al., 1985). The sphere of influence of the lay health workers does not stop with behaviors of at-risk individuals. Working through the social support networks of congregations, lay health advisers can enhance the delivery systems of medical service institutions and the problem-solving capacity of the community (Eng & Hatch, 1991). The lay health advisers, by virtue of their health training, serve as educators to fellow parishioners. This is done informally on a one-on-one basis and may also be accomplished by conducting classes within the church building. After proper training, the lay health advisers may also play an active role in screening, such as measuring blood pressure in a hypertension intervention. The responsibility for leading the recruitment of church members to classes and screenings falls on the lay health advisers (Davis et al., 1994). They also work together with local health providers to organize the activities within the church.

Eng et al. (1985) stress the importance of giving the lay health workers decision-making power in the design and execution of the intervention. This helps the project become institutionalized within the church and ensures its longevity. For the insights of the lay health advisers to be valued and used, health providers must accept the lay health advisers as colleagues and see them as influentials who can help promote health (Eng & Hatch, 1991). Hatch and Lovelace (1980) described an example in which the perceptiveness of the lay health advisers was employed. Health professionals determined that the needs of a particular community required an intervention to focus on hypertension, diabetes, and maternal and child health. The lay health workers also requested training to help them deal with cases of alcoholism and child abuse. They felt that these problems were prevalent in their community. Their suggestions were valued and incorporated into the education curriculum of the intervention.

The Selection of Lay Health Advisers

The success of a collaborative health intervention with a religious institution requires careful selection of the lay health advisers. These men and women must have a number of characteristics to perform their duties to the fullest. Perhaps the most vital quality of lay health advisers is that they are already active in the social support networks of the church. Lay health advisers are persons whom others in the congregation already trust, respect, and turn to for advice, support, and assistance. Examples of the type of daily help they provide to their fellow parishioners are day care assistance for children and older persons; counseling and emotional support on personal, family, and monetary matters; and connecting church members with each other or outside agencies with the experience and resources to assist with a particular problem. The nature of the help continually provided by potential lay health advisers is so spontaneous and informal that they may not be aware of the assistance they are providing (Eng & Hatch, 1991). Eng and Hatch shared the description of these natural helpers as offered by clergy and church members in one project, as "persons who are trusted for maintaining confidentiality, who listen with an open ear and caring heart, and who are respected for being sufficiently in control of their own life circumstances" (pp. 130-131). Natural helpers are usually influential members of social support networks within the black church (Eng et al., 1985). They are often involved in church and community activities and are respected by church members of all ages (Hatch & Lovelace, 1980).

Factors other than personality characteristics also play a role in the selection of lay health advisers. Individuals selected to serve as lay health advisers must be interested in the intervention and willing to participate (Eng & Hatch, 1991). Practical matters such as availability of time and the likelihood of the person's moving away from the community also need to be considered. Organizers need to state clearly and precisely the necessary time commitment volunteers need to make at the start of the project. In one intervention, the organizers stated from the beginning that the volunteer must be available at least one night a week for 12 weeks and must plan to stay in the community for at least 2 years (Hatch & Lovelace, 1980).

The minister, his or her assistants, or church officials play a key role in identifying the lay health advisers. After the pastor or person knowledgeable about the congregation is informed of the qualities desired in the prospective volunteer and the time commitment involved, he or she draws up a list of names of possible individuals to be recruited. From this list, individuals are selected on the basis of their interest and availability. Davis et al. (1994) described an intervention with a slightly more sophisticated procedure to select a lay health leader. They looked for a person with three attributes thought to enable a person to influence others in a group: the ability to project a positive self-image, ease and competence in communicating with other group members, and being accepted and respected as a group member. They drew up a list of 18 items that described the three characteristics. The pastor was asked to choose three possible lay health advisers and then to determine which person best characterized each item. Whichever individual was named most frequently by the pastor for the 18 items was selected as the lay health leader. The minister was given the right to have final say over the selection and to state whether the two top scorers should serve as a team. After the lay health advisers are selected, organizers must focus on their training.

The Training of Lay Health Advisers

The curriculum for the training of lay health advisers consists of medical information, strategies for working with other parishioners, and practical skills necessary to successfully fulfill their roles in health interventions. The number of training sessions that a project requires naturally varies according to the material that needs to be covered. Often, a different local private or public health professional speaks at each training session. Davis et al. (1994) limited their training sessions to 45 minutes and served refreshments to maximize attendance. If the intervention is expected to last for a considerable period, then booster sessions and repetition of the training sessions in cycles are necessary to maintain a well-trained group of lay health advisers.

The medical information shared during the training of the lay health advisers depends on the nature of the illness addressed by the intervention. Generally, it consists of a description of the nature and prevalence of the illness, facts on screening, and information about the importance of medical follow-up for any abnormalities. Lay health advisers also may be taught basic medical skills, such as how to measure blood pressure. Available community resources pertinent to the intervention are discussed in the training sessions. Lay health advisers are taught how to make referrals and thus connect parishioners in need with a professional or service agency that can assist them.

Much of the training of lay health advisers focuses on useful strategies to promote healthy behavior among the congregation. Methods of encouraging other church members to become actively involved in the intervention or in the recruitment of individuals for screenings are discussed (Davis et al., 1994). The lay health advisers may be instructed on strategies to encourage fellow parishioners to follow their physicians' orders or the prescribed regimens of their local health providers. They may also learn strategies to provide input to local health professionals and service agencies on how to better serve the needs of the local community (Hatch & Lovelace, 1980).

Other practical training may also be essential for the lay health advisers to properly fulfill their roles. They may be instructed in some basic counseling skills. Training may include communication techniques, such as how to deliver messages with confidence. Role play can be used to learn these techniques and to practice sharing health messages with other parishioners (Davis et al., 1994). The curriculum may also include instruction on how to organize events, a skill useful for planning screenings, health fairs, and meetings (Eng & Hatch, 1991).

Lay health advisers may also need to learn about the audiovisual equipment to be used in educating their fellow parishioners (Hatch & Lovelace, 1980).

Materials may be devised that are helpful to the lay health advisers either for their own education or in their efforts to share information with others. Leadership handbooks, brochures, and tip sheets can all be useful in providing guidance to the lay health advisers. These need to be written clearly and at a reading level suitable to that of the lay health advisers. Slide kits and other audiovisual material may be provided to the lay health advisers to assist them in sharing information with the rest of the congregation (Davis et al., 1994).

EXAMPLES OF HYPERTENSION INTERVENTIONS

Hypertension interventions are the most common black church-based health interventions. This is due to a number of reasons such as the relatively high prevalence of hypertension among African Americans as compared with whites; the ease of screening; and the large health benefits of detection, education, and behavioral change. Some of the church-based interventions are designed to address more than one health problem. For example, an intervention may focus on hypertension, diabetes, and maternal and child health. Sometimes, multiple health problems are addressed from the beginning of the intervention, and, at other times, illnesses are added through time as the program becomes established. Despite the dearth of reliable health data on black Seventh-Day Adventists, many black Seventh-Day Adventist pastors and church members are involved in educating their churches and communities about healthful living. Blacks in the Washington, D.C., area have access to Dr. Samuel DeShay's PLUS 15 program, a 15-day, medically controlled lifestyle approach to the treatment of high blood pressure and high blood cholesterol, without the use of drugs. Built on health principles gleaned from the Bible and the Spirit of the Prophecy, PLUS 15 has benefited thousands since it began in 1985 (Rock, 1996).

The other hypertension interventions presented in this section are of interest for different reasons. The first was initiated by a pastor and influenced the development of the second, larger program. Challenges met in working with lay health advisers are detailed in the third intervention. The final intervention has been described as the "most comprehensive, publicized, longstanding, and successful black church-based health program" (Levin, 1984, p. 481). According to Levin, one of the explicit goals of those who designed the interventions was to tap into the existing help networks in the black church through the lay health advisers and to use the networks to encourage and reinforce healthy behavior.

Williams and Williams (1984) reported the case of the maverick Reverend Melvin Charles Smith, who, in the early 1960s, noticed high levels of morbidity and mortality among his congregation at the Mount Moriah East Baptist Church in Memphis, Tennessee. Reverend Smith earned a B.S. in biology and studied theology at the graduate level. Many of his parishioners had not received professional medical care in 20 to 25 years. The reasons for their not seeking professional medical attention included lack of money and insurance, fear, and reliance on traditional remedies. He organized those in his church with medical expertise to provide free medical services to church members and members of the local community. One of the main foci of the program was to improve the parishioners' diets.

In 1977, Reverend Smith began to organize blood pressure checks after each church service (Williams & Williams, 1984). This screening, combined with health education lectures, lowered blood pressure and improved the health of his congregation. Stop smoking and exercise programs were also initiated. Reverend Smith's program spread to other churches in the Memphis area through the University of Tennessee Medical School and nationally through the National Red Cross Task Force.

In 1977, the University of Tennessee College of Medicine's Department of Community Medicine called together those involved locally in blood pressure screening and referral to discuss ways to improve blood pressure services in and around Memphis (Levin, 1984; Perry, 1981). The meeting included local religious leaders; a medical anthropologist; representatives from the local health department; the Memphis Association of Occupational Nurses; the Mid-South Health Professionals; the Community Action Agency (Orange Mound Health Center); and local affiliates of the American Heart Association, the Red Cross, and the Kidney Foundation. The committee consulted and arrived at a consensus that the best approach to improving blood pressure services would be to begin church-based interventions.

The committee decided to focus on 250 of the 800 black churches in Memphis and Shelby County. The combined membership of the 250 churches was approximately 80,000, or about 26% of the African American population in the area (Perry, 1981). The primary goal of the program was to improve the identification, referral, and maintenance of persons with hypertension (Levin, 1984). Volunteers from each involved church were taught basic knowledge about hypertension and its effects and were trained and certified as blood pressure technicians. Educational activities to encourage risk-reducing behavioral change were also conducted in the churches. Follow-up was facilitated by the use of church directories to contact those with high blood pressure who needed regular checking. This program served as a model for interventions in Cleveland, Detroit, Maryland, Mississippi, and rural Tennessee (Perry, 1981).

An intervention labeled the Churches as Hypertension Control Centers Program was instituted in Baltimore in 1979 (Kumanyika & Charleston, 1992). The program was organized by the Maryland High Blood Pressure Coordinating Council and the local affiliate of the American Heart Association and was funded by the National Heart, Lung, and Blood Institute (Levin, 1984). This intervention also screened for elevated blood pressure, referred individuals to physicians when necessary, performed follow-up checks as required, and provided relevant health education. The pastors of all black churches in the area were sent letters, and eventually 100 of 260 churches became hypertension control centers. The existence and purpose of the program were advertised at the beginning through television, radio, newspapers, and ministerial groups. Five hundred church volunteers were trained as blood pressure measurement specialists. They educated, screened, and monitored fellow parishioners (Kong et al., 1982). Another major church initiative in Baltimore involved 230 churches organized under the name of Clergy United for the Renewal of East Baltimore (CURE). This effort focuses directly on social, physical, mental, and spiritual needs of inner-city residents and has reached thousands through health promotion programs, health links, substance abuse programs, and other initiatives.

One initiative developed into the Heart, Body, and Soul Program. This program is a partnership among CURE, Johns Hopkins Center for Health Program, the health department of Baltimore City, community groups, and churches. The program opened three preventive centers in the community to provide blood pressure, cholesterol, vision, and carbon monoxide screenings; nutrition evaluations; tuberculosis tests; and referrals for mammograms. These centers, along with church-based health fairs, have enabled thousands of people to receive free health services and screening. Health fairs are held two to three times a month in area churches after the Sunday morning service and at schools and grocery stores (Tuggle, 1995).

The final hypertension intervention offered as an example of a collaborative intervention between religious institutions and health professionals is the Health and Human Services Project initiated in 1980 by the North Carolina General Baptist State Convention (GBSC; Hatch & Jackson, 1981; Levin, 1984). It received its initial funding from the Kellogg and the Z. Smith Reynolds Foundations. The GBSC agreed to take over the funding after the grants ended (Eng & Hatch, 1991). The aim of this project was to reduce morbidity and mortality associated with hypertension, diabetes, and maternal and child health. Lay health advisers were to use the social networks of the churches to encourage self-care and healthy behavior. Their role also encompassed screening, counseling, and providing social support (Levin, 1984). The potential outreach of this project was massive, with the GBSC's 1,700 black churches and 400,000 adult members (Hatch & Jackson, 1981).

Eng and Hatch (1991) described how the GBSC administered this gigantic program. The GBSC hired three public health professionals: one health administrator and two health educators on a full-time basis. These three staff members had a number of responsibilities. Each year, the staff and the GBSC leadership targeted 10 to 20 churches in the same geographical region to be initiated into the intervention. The staff worked with the churches to select the lay health advisers and recruited local public and private health professionals to train them. The three staff members were responsible for establishing the link between the lay health advisers and the local health professionals and service agencies. They also served as consultants to the lay health advisers on how to organize activities and request technical support from health and service agencies.

Eng and Hatch (1991) briefly outlined the success of the program. At the end of 5 years, the GBSC had initiated the program in all its districts. Evaluation has shown an increase in knowledge and use of services and a decrease in health risks among parishioners of the churches involved in the intervention. The GBSC assumed complete financial responsibility for the intervention. A GBSC board was formed to oversee the program. Health education materials were handled by the GBSC Christian Education Office. The church-based public health intervention of the GBSC has won a national award from the U.S. Department of Health and Human Services for being one of the most innovative health promotion programs and a state award from the Governor's Office for excellence in community service.

EXAMPLES OF
NONHYPERTENSION INTERVENTIONS

Collaborative interventions between religious institutions and health professionals are quite versatile. Such interventions can have a significant impact on public health problems other than hypertension. This section describes interventions that focus on diabetes, cervical cancer, cholesterol, diet, and mutual help groups among caregivers to older persons. These examples demonstrate that church-based programs have the potential to alleviate many health problems in the black community.

Diabetes

In 1994, the American Diabetes Association began a collaborative intervention with black churches in the Los Angeles area to increase awareness and knowledge of diabetes among African Americans ("Black Church Diabetes Education," 1994; "Black Church Diabetes Program," 1994). The Black Church Diabetes Education Program encompassed 200 churches and was funded by Blue Cross of California. The program was aimed at encouraging church members who have diabetes or are at risk of developing diabetes to seek information and treatment. Early detection increases the chances that diabetes and blood sugar levels can be controlled and decreases the risks of serious complications.

Dr. Bill Releford, chairman of the American Diabetes Association's African American Outreach Committee, explained why a church-based program was developed. He said,

> It is an ideal vehicle for this program because it reaches those without access to other sources of information and serves as a non-threatening link between members and the wider community. In addition, African Americans historically have turned to the Church for health and healing purposes. ("Black Church Diabetes Education," 1994, p. 1)

Cancer

In the early 1990s, researchers from the Charles R. Drew University of Medicine and Science in Los Angeles started a church-based cervical cancer control program with 23 black and Latino churches in south and south central Los Angeles (Davis et al., 1994). The Drew University campus of the Drew-Meharry-Morehouse Consortium Cancer Center, the Central Los Angeles Unit of the American Cancer Society, and the Association of Black Women Physicians were involved in the project. The goal of the program was to evaluate the efficacy of using church-based programs to increase access to and participation of minority women in cervical cancer control.

Female church members age 21 and older were eligible for the educational and screening components of the cervical cancer control intervention (Davis et al., 1994). The 1-hour educational sessions were held directly after worship services in large halls in the churches. Information was shared at the sessions, question-and-answer periods were held, and participants were asked to complete questionnaires that included their screening histories. Women who indicated in their survey responses that they had not had a Papanicolaou (Pap) test within the last 2 years were eligible for a free test. The churches also provided secluded rooms with doors where the Pap tests were conducted. Two nurse practitioners performed the screenings at each church site. They were provided with all the necessary supplies, including gurneys and screens.

Analysis of the surveys conducted at the educational session showed substantial differences between the African American and Hispanic women who participated in the intervention (Davis et al., 1994). The black women were of higher socioeconomic status than the Latinas. They reported an average annual income of $20,000 to $24,999, compared with the Latinas' $7,500 to $9,999. The black participants also had a much higher educational level. Black women were 6.6 times more likely than the Latinas to have had a Pap test in the last

2 years. During the question-and-answer period, some black women expressed their discomfort with the free screenings. They felt that they did not want to be treated as poor and said that in the black community, *free* often signifies substandard services. Davis et al. suggest that charging a fee for the screenings should be evaluated on a church-by-church basis in consultation with the lay health leaders.

Davis et al. (1994) concluded that the use of social networks through lay health leaders in church-based cancer control programs can increase the participation of underserved minorities. During the study, 1,012 women attended the educational sessions, and 490 received a Pap test. Of the women tested, 10% had abnormal smears, and follow-up care was arranged for them. Two years after the end of the initial study, 52% of the churches involved were continuing in cancer control activities.

Cholesterol

Wiist and Flack (1990) performed a pilot study to determine the applicability of a dietary education program to lower serum cholesterol in individuals in black churches with classes taught by lay volunteers. The study was performed in a city in the southwestern United States with support from the National Institutes of Health; the National Heart, Lung, and Blood Institute; Pfizer Pharmaceutical; the Oklahoma City-County Health Department; and the Oklahoma State Health Department. In this investigation, Wiist and Flack planned to compare the reduction in cholesterol levels between individuals screened with high cholesterol who attended dietary education classes and those who had a copy of their results sent to their personal physicians—the "usual care" group. Wiist and Flack pointed out that despite the high rates of heart disease among African Americans, little research has been conducted to determine the effect of educational interventions on behavioral risk factors among blacks. This is especially true with regard to diet and cholesterol.

Wiist and Flack (1990) found that after 6 months, both the usual care group and the education group had reduced their cholesterol significantly. Surprisingly, they also found that the usual care group reduced their cholesterol levels more than the education group. Wiist and Flack concluded that church-based cholesterol educational interventions with lay volunteer instructors are an effective method of lowering cholesterol in the black community. They note that although collaborating with black churches enables the reaching of large numbers of blacks, other efforts should also be made to reach African Americans who do not attend religious services, such as through the public library. Other locations to conduct screenings include beauty and barber shops, meetings/functions of social, civic, and public service organizations, and sports and entertainment venues.

Diet

The lead author (Braithwaite) and a colleague (Dr. Ken Resnicow) are recipients of a 5-year National Cancer Institute research program called Eat for Life. Eat for Life is a multicomponent intervention designed to increase fruit and vegetable consumption among African Americans that is delivered through black churches in the Atlanta metropolitan area.

Fourteen churches were randomly assigned to one of three treatment conditions: (1) comparison (usual nutrition education), (2) culturally sensitive multicomponent intervention with one phone call, and (3) culturally sensitive multicomponent intervention with four phone calls. The intervention included an 18-minute video, a project cookbook, printed health education materials, including a quarterly newsletter, and several "cues" imprinted with the project logo and a 5-a-day message. A key element of the telephone intervention is the use of *motivational interviewing,* a counseling technique originally developed for addictive behaviors that has potential application to other health behaviors. Major outcomes for the trial include total fruit and vegetable intake (assessed by three food frequency questionnaires and 24-hour recalls) and serum carotenoids. Psychosocial variables assessed include outcome expectations, barriers to fruit and vegetable intake, preference for meat meals, neophobia, social support to eat more fruits and vegetables, self-efficacy to eat more fruits and vegetables, perceived need to eat more fruits and vegetables, and nutrition knowledge.

Baseline means fruits and vegetables intake across the three food frequency questionnaires ranged from 3.64 to 4.44. The psychosocial variable most strongly correlated ($r = .39$) with fruit and vegetable intake was self-efficacy. Other variables positively correlated with fruit and vegetable intake included outcome expectations, social support, and low-fat cooking practices. Factors negatively correlated with intake included perceived barriers, perceived need to eat more fruit and vegetables, meat preference, neophobia, and high-fat cooking practices. Approximately 40% of the variance in fruit and vegetable intake was accounted for by demographic, behavioral, and psychosocial variables. Eat for Life represents a potentially effective intervention for increasing fruit and vegetable intake among African Americans. Efficacy of the intervention will be determined at the 1-year follow-up.

Mutual Help Groups for Caregivers

The final example of a health intervention that resulted from a collaboration between health professionals and religious institutions is the founding of mutual help groups among individuals active in the care of older persons. This example demonstrates more of the diversity of programs that can be initiated through cooperation between health workers and religious leaders. Staff members from the Institute of Gerontology at the University of the District of Columbia worked with eight black churches to develop mutual help groups at each church site (Haber, 1983).

Haber (1983) described the three components of the project: training of group members, starting up the group, and evaluation. Each church formed a class of approximately 25 to 30 parishioners who were actively involved in the care of frail older persons. Training consisted of 12 hours of instruction. The curriculum covered a wide range of topics such as chronic illnesses and behavioral change with age, basic nursing skills for caring for older persons at home, the psychology of aging, sensory deprivation, and communication with older persons. It also included alternative living arrangements and community resources. After the classes were completed, staff from the Institute of Gerontology helped initiate the mutual help groups. The staff members provided each group member with a comprehensive directory of resources available to assist him or her in caring for older persons. Members were also taught how to use the directory and keep it up to date. A list of fellow church members who could be used as resources or were available to assist older persons was also disseminated to the members of the mutual help groups.

Haber (1983) noted a number of accomplishments of the mutual help groups. They sponsored activities such as educational seminars, film presentations, discussion groups, and classes in the writing of a will and testament. A newsletter was established. Fundraisers were held to build a ramp in front of a church. Transportation to and from church services for older persons was improved. The one shortcoming noted is that the caregivers' mutual help groups were not becoming self-sustaining after staff members from the Institute of Gerontology stopped providing direction, assistance, and support. Within 3 months after the training program, two of the mutual help groups had already dissolved. Research can be conducted on factors that affect the longevity of mutual help groups. The need for this type of program for caregivers to older persons may increase as population aging continues. This may be true especially for the black community in the United States, where the absolute and relative numbers of old persons who are black are expected to increase (U.S. Department of Commerce, 1993).

LIMITATIONS OF COLLABORATING WITH BLACK RELIGIOUS INSTITUTIONS

Limitations that health professionals have found while working with religious institutions on collaborative health projects have been identified in the literature. For example, while trying to promote maternal and child health programs among poor urban churches, church representatives reported to Olson et al.

(1988) that they believed a shortage of volunteers, funds, church staff time to manage a program, and assistance by private and government agencies would make implementation of a program difficult. One of the criticisms of service agencies involved in collaborative interventions from the perspective of churches is that frequent changes of liaison staff make it difficult to maintain linkages (Morrison, 1991). Two of the most common limitations, lack of male participation and discomfort of churches with interventions focusing on sexuality and drug abuse, are addressed below.

Health professionals generally find that collaborating with black religious institutions is an effective form of outreach. One shortcoming noted in many studies is a lack of participation by black men, especially young black men. For example, Kumanyika and Charleston (1992) found it difficult to recruit black men for weight loss classes that were part of a blood pressure control program even when separate classes were organized for men. Given that hypertension is a serious health threat to young black men, the lack of participation among this group is a particular challenge. These men are less likely than others to avail themselves of the benefits of screening and diagnosis or to see a physician after referral (Kong et al., 1982). Eng et al. (1985) explain that the lack of participation by black men is attributable to different help-seeking patterns, the history of race relations, and conflicting expectations in the patient-provider relationship. Another reason that black men participate less than black women in church-based health interventions is that black men are less likely than black women to attend and to be active in church services and programs (Levin & Taylor, 1993). One method to compensate for this problem and to encourage male participation is to insist that when lay health advisers are selected, at least one of them is a man. Otherwise, in many cases, only women are chosen to serve as lay health advisers (Eng & Hatch, 1991; Hatch & Jackson, 1981). It is believed that women who are active in church and participate in health education projects can influence the health behavior of their male relatives through education and encouragement (Eng et al., 1985; Kong et al., 1982). The efficacy of reaching black men through significant women in their lives needs to be investigated.

Another limitation of collaborating with religious institutions on health interventions is that the churches are often uncomfortable dealing with health issues related to sexuality and drug behavior (Thomas et al., 1994). Harm reduction interventions such as distributing condoms and clean needles are perceived as condoning behavior that contradicts religious teachings (Thomas & Quinn, 1993). Thomas et al. (1994) point out not only that churches are reluctant to deal with these sensitive topics but also that substantial opposition to condom and needle distribution has been organized by black church leaders. Black clergy have argued against these programs on moral and genocidal grounds (Thomas & Quinn, 1993). "Giving needles to addicts is actually helping those persons to kill themselves" and the proponents of needle exchange programs "are perpetuating a system of black genocide" are two examples of statements by black ministers that illustrate their perspective (p. 334).

A study by Rubin et al. (1994) quantifies the shortage of programs resulting from the reluctance of black religious institutions to address health issues related to sexuality and drug abuse. Surveying 635 northern black churches, Rubin et al. found that 176 sponsored youth programs aimed primarily at nonmember youths from low-income homes. Of these 176 churches, 27 had parenting/sexuality and substance abuse programs, 6 had youth AIDS support programs, and only 4 had youth health-related programs. Rubin et al. conclude that some of the most serious problems facing black youth were not being addressed by black churches.

Strategies have been devised to deal with the reluctance of religious institutions to get involved in health projects dealing with sexuality and drug abuse. Some authors propose that public health professionals should attempt to collaborate with religious institutions only on projects that are harmonious with their missions and should work with secular agencies on controversial projects (Eng et al., 1985; Thomas et al., 1994). Another approach is to package the intervention in a manner acceptable to the religious organization. Hence, having a biblical basis for the health or change intervention strategy is crucial. For example, the Eat for Life program builds its foundation on scriptures. According to the scripture and commentary on portions of the Old Testament, it appears that the ideal diet for humans' optimal health is one that consists of vegetarian foods. Several verses in the New Testament state the importance of keeping the body in good health:

> Know ye not that ye are the temple of God, and that the Spirit of God dwelleth in you? If any man defile the temple of God, him shall God destroy; for the temple of God is holy, which temple ye are. (1 Cor. 3:16-17, King James Version)
>
> I beseech you therefore, brethren, by the mercies of God, that ye present your bodies a living sacrifice, holy, acceptable unto God, which is your reasonable service. (Romans 12:1)
>
> Whether therefore ye eat, or drink, or whatsoever ye do, do all to the glory of God. (1 Cor. 10:31)
>
> What? Know ye not that your body is the temple of the Holy Ghost which is in you, which ye have of God, and ye are not your own? For ye are bought with a price; therefore glorify God in your body, and in your spirit, which are God's. (1 Cor. 6:19-20)

Eng and Hatch (1991) wrote that they approached the problem of teenage pregnancy in a church-based intervention by addressing it in the context of maternal and child health to avoid difficulties with the sensitive topic of premarital sexual relations. From a different angle, Allen-Meares (1989) openly advocates that black churches become involved in sex education for children and adolescents. She believes that the churches could reduce premature sexual activity and pregnancies. McAdoo and Crawford (1990) state that some churches have found themselves forced to deal with issues related to sexuality and drug abuse because of the magnitude of the social problems they cause. They report that churches have become sophisticated in allowing outside groups that address these problems to use their facilities. Still, McAdoo and Crawford conclude that most churches have yet to resolve how to confront issues related to sexuality, HIV, and drug abuse. Critical to the discussion on how to make contact with hard-to-reach populations is the medium of communication. Youth must be talked with in a language they understand and embrace. For example, Stephens, Braithwaite, and Taylor (1998) describe a model for use of hip-hop music in small groups as a strategy for HIV prevention counseling with African American adolescents and young adults.

The foregoing examples of health interventions are intended to be helpful for those considering development of collaborative health projects. Interventions can be large and long-term or as simple as an annual health fair that screens for various health problems. Their variety is demonstrated by the above examples of interventions that address hypertension, diabetes, cervical cancer, cholesterol, diet, and mutual help groups among caregivers of older persons. Ingenuity can lead to discovering new ways of working with the black faith community to improve the health of African Americans.

Collaborative health interventions are beneficial to the work of both religious leaders and public health professionals. For the churches, such projects offer an opportunity to directly serve the needs of the black community and fulfill their healing and service missions. The resources of religious institutions are complemented by the medical expertise and organizational skills of health professionals. Health professionals have found working with churches an effective form of outreach to the black community. The churches provide them with material and human resources as well as legitimacy. Lay health advisers can be instrumental in helping initiate and maintain behavioral change that reduces risk behavior. Limitations of collaborations between religious institutions and health workers, such as relatively low male participation and avoidance by churches of dealing with issues related to sexuality and drug abuse, need to be kept in mind. The main beneficiary of religious institutions and health professionals working together is the greater black community. Working together, they improve the health of African Americans and decrease the health disparity between blacks and whites.

6

Communities of Color Respond to Environmental Threats to Health

The Environmental Justice Framework

Environmental hazards pose serious health threats in many ethnic minority and low-income communities in general, and in African American communities in particular. Substantial evidence has been documented to show that communities of color are exposed to a disproportionate amount of environmental hazards. This translates into greater health risks for ethnic minority and low-income citizens. The differential distribution of environmental hazards and health burdens has given birth to an environmental justice movement that seeks to galvanize people of color to fight the inequities that affect their health status and quality of life. Environmental justice and equity advocacy groups have organized and successfully fought local hazards, demonstrating that African Americans have taken and are taking an active role in responding to the environmental issues that affect their survival (Freudenberg, 1984; Taylor, 1989, 1992). Furthermore, these groups rely on community organization tactics and coalition building to bring about the desired changes.

The purpose of this chapter is to explore how African American communities are responding to environmental threats to their health and well-being via coalition methods. We will present research on the relationship between the incidence of environmental hazards and race, give an overview of the development of black environmentalism, and discuss examples of grassroots organizations and coalitions in African American communities that have formed in response to environmental injustices. This chapter will show how some communities have perceived environmental threats to health, what strategies have been employed, and what outcomes have resulted from their efforts. By reviewing the literature and the accounts of citizens actively fighting to protect their environment and health, we seek to provide practical information on how people of color, specifically African Americans, can use community organization and coalition-building techniques to address environmental problems and promote health.

A QUESTION OF ENVIRONMENTAL RACISM

Environmental equity implies that both environmental hazards and protection from hazards are distributed equally. In the early 1980s, as African Americans began to focus on environmental hazards as a civil rights issue, anecdotal evidence implied that environmental protection was not equitably distributed. Instead, African American neighborhoods and other communities of color seemed to be more severely affected by environmental burdens. After the first national black protest of a hazardous waste facility, Reverend Benjamin F. Chavis coined the phrase *environmental racism* to refer to the racial discrimination in environmental policy, enforcement of laws and regulations, and the siting of environmentally hazardous and unwanted land uses that creates the inequitable distribution (U.S. Congress, 1994). Since that time, environmental racism has become a key concept in the struggle of African Americans against environmental threats to health and survival. It has changed the dialogue from one of equity to one of justice.

Several studies have explored the relationship between race and environmental hazards (Bullard, 1992, 1993, 1994a). It has been difficult to determine whether the distribution of hazards is related to socioeconomic status, which often reflects racial stratification in the United States, or race itself. Substantial evidence indicates that race does play a significant role in the distribution of environmental hazards and protection, as demonstrated by the following three studies. At the request of Congressman Walter E. Fauntroy, who participated in the Warren County protest (to be discussed later), the U.S. General Accounting Office (GAO; 1988) conducted a study that found that three of the four off-site hazardous waste landfills in the Southeast were located in predominantly poor African American communities. This report prompted another landmark study, *Toxic Wastes and Race in the United States,* by the United Church of Christ Commission for Racial Justice (1987), to identify national patterns of landfill distribution on the basis of zip codes. The commission's study found that although low socioeconomic status was related to the existence of commercial hazardous waste facilities in a community, the racial composition of the community was the best indicator of the location of waste facilities. It concluded that it was virtually impossible for the disproportionate distribution of facilities in African American communities to have occurred by chance. In the third study, Mohai and Bryant (1992) conducted a meta-analysis of 15 existing studies on environmental hazards, race, and income and carried out a study of their own in Detroit. They conclude that although both racial and class biases exist, race is an independent and perhaps more significant variable in determining distribution of environmental hazards.

Studies documenting evidence of racial and economic bias in the distribution of environmental hazards have been available since the early 1970s (Mohai & Bryant, 1992). Public awareness of environmental justice issues, however, did not occur until much later. More recent studies continue to examine the evidence of environmental racism. A comprehensive study by the *National Law Journal* looked at the legal and regulation enforcement dimensions of the environmental justice issue (Lavelle & Coyle, 1992). After reviewing every U.S. environmental lawsuit in a 7-year period, they found that penalties imposed on polluters in minority areas are less severe than penalties imposed on facilities in white areas. They also found that the government was slower (by 20%) to initiate cleanup of Superfund sites in minority communities.

Some investigators, however, question the environmental inequity evidence. Anderton, Anderson, Rossi, et al. (1994) and Anderton, Anderson, Oakes, and Fraser (1994) conducted at the Social and Demographic Research Institute the first national study of hazardous waste facilities using census tract-level data. Their studies found no significant differences in race or ethnic composition between census tracts containing a waste facility and those tracts with none. An important point raised by this work is that distribution patterns differ depending on the unit of analysis chosen in the methodology.

The GAO (1995a) found similar results in a study of the race and income of people living near a sample of nonhazardous municipal landfills. The percentage of ethnic minorities and low-income people living within a mile of municipal landfills was not higher than the percentage in the rest of the county. Another GAO publication (1995b) summarized 10 studies published since 1986 that addressed hazardous waste facilities on a regional or national level. The results of the studies varied greatly in the importance of race and income as indicators of the distribution of hazardous waste sites.

Many gaps still exist in the research. For example, the distribution of environmental hazards such as water pollution have not been studied, as well as air pollution and hazardous waste disposal (Mohai & Bryant, 1992). Also, current knowledge about the health impact of these environmental hazards continues to be refined. Nevertheless, the majority of existing research tends to support the conclusion that race, independently of class, plays a significant role in the distribution of environmental hazards and protection.

DEVELOPMENT OF BLACK ENVIRONMENTALISM

The development of the environmental movement is perhaps the most obvious way in which concerned citizens have attempted to respond to the environmental hazards that threaten health and the quality of life. The history of the movement, however, reveals that people of color were conspicuously absent from environmental activist groups (Baugh, 1991). Only during the most recent phase, which began in the 1980s, did black environmentalism emerge. Since then, this new type of environmentalism has become a powerful tool for coping with the environmental problems in communities of color.

Numerous debates exist about the lack of minority involvement in environmental organizations. One argument that has received a lot of attention is that blacks are "less interested, concerned, and informed about the natural environment than whites" (Taylor, 1989, p. 179). History and research, however, have challenged the "concern gap" explanation. Taylor demonstrates that the observed pattern of minimal concern can be attributed to the use of inappropriate indicator measures and unrepresentative sampling techniques in previous studies. In Bullard's (1994a) study of five African American communities (both low- and middle-income), concern for the environment was often rated by residents as more important than concern for jobs, contradicting the popular argument that African Americans favor economic growth over environmental protection. Finally, the numerous examples of African American community organization efforts against local environmental hazards since the 1980s testify that blacks are concerned about the environmental issues that affect their communities (Bernstein et al., 1994; Bullard, 1993, 1994a, 1994b; Capek, 1993; EPA, 1992a; Freudenberg, 1984).

An alternative argument explaining the lack of minority involvement in the environmental movement is the mainstream movement's neglect of issues such as housing, education, and unemployment that are relevant to communities of color (Baugh, 1991). Mainstream organizations are frequently accused of ignoring environmental issues when there are problems in poor and minority areas. This has given rise to the "not in my backyard" (NIMBY) attitude behind many of the mainstream environmental efforts. A related concern is that mainstream environmentalists focus on less relevant problems while distracting attention and resources from higher-priority problems such as racism, poverty, and economic development (Baugh, 1991; Taylor, 1989). Moreover, according to Baugh, mainstream environmental organizations have been accused of institutional racism because of their poor record of hiring and promoting minority professionals. Clearly, the structure and narrow agendas of mainstream environmental organizations have hindered black participation.

Despite the obstacles to participation in mainstream environmental movements, people of color have developed methods and strategies for dealing with environmental threats. These methods have formed the basis for the third environmental movement.

This new brand of environmentalism became nationally publicized in 1982 by events in Warren County, North Carolina (Bullard, 1994a; Freudenberg, 1984; Lee, 1993). For 4 years, residents of predominantly African American Warren County protested the state's plan to dump soil laced with highly toxic polychlorinated biphenyl (PCB) in a landfill proximate to dwellings for residents of this county. The PCB was dumped illegally along roads, resulting in the largest PCB spill ever documented. The contaminated soil was left along the roadways for 4 years while the state selected a site to bury the soil. The selection of Warren County as the burial site has been described as based on political motives rather than scientifically sound reasons. In 1982, after approaching the United Church of Christ Commission for Racial Justice, local residents were joined by civil rights leaders, environmental activists, labor leaders, and black elected officials. The ensuing protest campaign included tactics such as lying in streets to block the entrance of trucks carrying the soil into the landfill. The nonviolent civil disobedience resulted in more than 500 arrests (United Church of Christ Commission for Racial Justice, 1987).

These events are recognized as the first national protest by African Americans against the issue of hazardous waste facility siting. Although the protesters were unsuccessful in stopping the burial of the soil in the landfill, the events did have several positive outcomes. It clearly linked environmental issues to civil rights, and it brought this relationship to national attention. As a result of the media exposure, the state reconsidered its landfill siting policies and enacted a 2-year moratorium on hazardous waste landfill siting. The event also generated interest in research on the relationship between race and toxic waste, which has formed the basis of environmental racism documentation (Lee, 1992).

Since the Warren County protest, myriad environmental justice groups have fought local hazards in ethnic minority communities. Although hazardous waste has been a popular focus, these groups have worked on many issues including lead poisoning, municipal landfills, air pollution, water contamination, and even natural disasters. Black environmental groups may differ in the issues and strategies chosen; they frequently stem, however, from an environmental justice framework. Environmental racism has become a key concept in this new approach to environmental protection. The use of the environmental racism paradigm allows the hazard to be examined within a framework of social justice. This new form of environmentalism has succeeded in attracting African Americans. Bullard (1994a) shows that grassroots, social action, and emergent coalition environmental groups have been more appealing than have mainstream environmental groups to black activists because of their concern about inequality, emphasis on direct action, and support for the economic and political underdog. These types of environmental groups, typical of the new environ-

mental movement, have used an environmental justice framework as a method
to protect and restore the quality of life in African American communities.

An important element of the environmental justice movement is the emphasis
on forming partnerships between grassroots organizations and decision makers.
The need for such coalitions has been recognized by community advocates and
federal agencies alike. In 1994, President Clinton issued Executive Order
12898, which directed federal agencies to develop strategies to address environmental and health conditions in ethnic minority and low-income communities. In response, the Environmental Protection Agency (EPA; 1995b) outlined
its strategy that recognized the importance of partnerships in enhancing community participation. Some of its proposed coalition partners are affected
communities, government agencies, academic institutions, business, and industry. Similarly, affected communities are demanding that their voices be included
in the dialogue that creates environmental priorities (Bullard, 1994b). Partnerships offer communities the opportunity to participate in identifying risks and
research gaps and developing action models. Such partnerships have successfully addressed lead abatement, pollution prevention, clean water, and safe
housing (EPA, 1995a). The literature is replete with examples of communities
of color that have formed coalitions and used grassroots organizing to preserve
environmental quality. To illustrate this framework, the following sections will
describe three recent community efforts to cope with environmental hazards.
Table 6.1 summarizes the features that are characteristic of the environmental
justice framework in the three case studies.

CASE 1: CHEMICAL POLLUTION
IN COLUMBIA, MISSISSIPPI

The Reichhold chemical plant was a polluting neighbor to the low-income
African American and white residents of Columbia for generations. For many
years, however, residents were unaware of the toxic chemicals to which they
were being exposed or of the toll the pollution was taking on the community.
On learning of the injustices committed by the corporation, local groups formed
to pursue legal compensation for the affected citizens. Some residents, however,
were frustrated by the failure of these groups to address the issue of social
justice for all residents of the community. To fill this need, an environmental
justice group known as Jesus People Against Pollution (JPAP) was created after
years of health problems, noxious fumes, and unexplained phenomena.

In 1975, an investigation by the Occupational Safety and Health Administration revealed that the company had been producing hazardous chemicals (a base
for Agent Orange) without a permit. The penalty imposed was a fine of $200.
Despite the investigation, residents were still not told about the types of chemicals being produced or alerted about the potential dangers, while Reichhold

TABLE 6.1 Summary of Case Studies Showing Aspects of the Environmental Justice Framework

	Columbia, Mississippi	*Southwest Atlanta, Georgia*	*Albany, Georgia*
Type of community	Low income, black and white	Middle income, black	Low income, black
Environmental issue	Hazardous chemical waste	Combined sewer overflow/wastewater treatment	Flood recovery
Leadership	Churches	Neighborhood planning groups	Political activists
Objective	Create an active community voice in cleanup	Implement community solution and discontinuation of current wastewater treatment policies	Investigate allegations, assist residents in recovery, rebuild neighborhoods
Strategies	Education, political action, direct action	Education, political action	Education and political, legal, and direct action
Coalition partners	Government agencies, universities, grassroots groups	Local environmental and political organizations	Service organizations, grassroots groups

continued to expel pollutants into the community. In 1977, a large explosion and fire forced Reichhold to abandon the site. As a result, the community was left to deal with more than 4,500 drums of chemicals buried in a field or simply left on flats at ground level.

For the next 9 years, the chemical waste issue was not addressed by the government, while residents complained of health problems, fish kills, and chemical ground fires related to the abandoned site. After pressure was exerted by the local civil defense director in 1986, the EPA designated the area a national priority Superfund site. Despite this progress, community residents were unhappy with the lack of citizen participation in cleanup planning and implementation. Residents also felt that their concerns were not being addressed. Although people witnessed an increase in cancers, birth defects, learning disabilities, and skin disorders, the government did little to inform residents about the risks posed by the site and the cleanup activities, nor was medical testing provided to measure exposure to toxins. In their attempts to be included in the discourse dominated by government and the corporation, community members experienced resistance from city, county, state, and federal officials. Rather than discussing the issues in a public forum, officials have attempted to cover up and downplay the magnitude of the problem.

Thus, the community was victimized first by Reichhold (the polluting corporation) and then by the government officials who failed to protect them. The founder and president of JPAP explained the situation by saying, "We are enslaved to the pollution problem of the corporations and the politicians" (C. Keys, personal communication, August 22, 1995). The function of JPAP is to serve as a voice for the poor and minority residents and as an advocate for the community. The group has many objectives: to educate community residents about health risks, to design a plan to relocate families living near the site, to establish medical services in the community, and to maintain a community voice in the cleanup. The JPAP employs a variety of educational, political, and direct action strategies to meet these goals. Previous and continuing activities include conducting a health survey of 20,000 residents, holding meetings, distributing newsletters, campaigning door-to-door, and visiting homes.

Coalition building and networking have enabled JPAP to draw on resources that are not available in the impoverished area. It has been the key to bringing all the responsible and affected parties to the same table. The JPAP has formed *partnership initiatives* or registered agreements with federal agencies, social institutions, and community groups to develop a model for collaborative problem solving. The Agency for Toxic Substances and Disease Registry, the CDC, the National Institute for Environmental Health Sciences, the EPA, national organizations, and universities are among their partners. Currently, JPAP is responsible for organizing a workshop involving many government agencies. Although community residents may find it difficult to regain their trust in government protection, the workshop will offer an opportunity to encourage cooperation between government agencies and grassroots groups. Other network-building activities promote community-to-community partnerships. Visiting speakers share their ideas and experiences with residents, and JPAP members travel to help organize and educate other communities facing similar threats.

Although the damage done by the pollution cannot be reversed, JPAP continues to bring about community improvements that alleviate the long-term losses. An example is JPAP's work with federal health agencies in the Mississippi Delta Project, which will pilot test the development of a community health center to address illnesses related to toxic exposure and access to primary health care. Other gains in community education and participation have been made, but JPAP's work is a continuing process that the group hopes can be used as a model for multisector cooperation and partnership worldwide.

CASE 2: WASTEWATER TREATMENT IN SOUTHWEST ATLANTA, GEORGIA

Not every community struggle is as well defined as JPAP's crusade against hazardous chemical waste in Columbia. For the residents of South Fulton

County in Atlanta, the environmental hazard includes the entire wastewater disposal and treatment system in their community. At first, the problem, visible sewage, was easy to pinpoint. As the residents looked deeper, however, they found that the problem became increasingly complex.

Five years ago, the chair of a neighborhood planning unit attended a meeting in which city planners announced a plan to build a system to transport sewage from north suburban communities to her community for treatment. Residents of the neighborhoods to be affected, in a predominantly African American middle-class area, were not aware of the plan. In response, the chair invited city officials to come to the next neighborhood meeting to discuss the plan with community residents. This was the residents' introduction to the wastewater issue that threatened the area.

Residents became more informed and learned of a plan to build a combined sewer overflow facility in a local park. Because Atlanta's sewage system is outdated, storm water combined with sewage would overflow into the park, producing an odor and a public health menace. Residents were unhappy with this plan to build a facility to treat sewage in a park where their children played. Instead, they proposed an alternative plan to separate the sewage from the storm water, thus eliminating the overflow problem. On reviewing the plan in detail, residents found funding and other discrepancies between the proposed facility in their park and another proposed facility to solve a similar problem in a predominantly white, middle-class neighborhood. Although few people claimed that the differences were the result of blatant racism, it was clear to many residents that more covert forms of institutional racism played a part in the differential treatment of the two communities.

The future of the park was not the only thing at stake. Residents learned that because of policies set in place 30 years ago, their community has unwittingly been responsible for treating much of the region's wastewater. The residents' perception of the problem has evolved as residents educate themselves about the complexities of the wastewater issue. The issue originated as a concern about the future of a local park, but since then, it has become an issue of environmental equity. Residents question, "What right does another community have to use our community as a waste disposal site or to accommodate a waste disposal system so they can continue to experience a superior quality of life without experiencing any of the problems?" (V. Watkins, personal communication, September 7, 1995). Part of the burden the community bears is increased health risks, documented in a study by the Fulton County Health Department (1995). This study found that residents were at increased risk for lung and other cancers, asthma, and other respiratory and pulmonary diseases. Additional burdens associated with the waste disposal system include devalued properties, damaged parks and public spaces, unpleasant odors, and an erosion of the quality of life.

The community's strategy to combat the perceived injustices depended on resident education, community solidarity, and ability to debate in public forums. Active residents attended city council meetings, studied papers introduced to relevant committees, and combated the city's continual attempts to convince citizens that the issues were too technical for them to comprehend. Coalition building and networking were essential to this process. The neighborhood planning unit members, block clubs, and other concerned community residents formed loose confederations with environmental and political organizations throughout the city on the basis of shared goals. The environmental groups were a valuable resource for community residents because of their history and experience in dealing with environmental issues and their strong networks and ability to lobby.

The result of the hard work and collaborative efforts was a victory at the city council. To date, however, the solution supported by the community has not been fully implemented, and sewage still overflows in the park. Moreover, no clear success has been gained in getting the city government to reconsider the wastewater treatment policies and philosophies that inequitably affect communities in Atlanta. The ultimate achievement has been the degree to which community residents have been able to assert their voice into the political dialogue on issues surrounding wastewater treatment.

This represents a limited use of community empowerment because underlying issues such as the lack of resources within the area have yet to be addressed (Bernstein et al., 1994). This community's experience with collective action, however, provides the basis for obtaining a level of community empowerment that will enable residents to participate in all issues affecting the well-being of the community.

CASE 3: FLOODS IN ALBANY, GEORGIA

The third case study is atypical of the types of environmental justice groups described in the literature. The problems, causes, and solutions this community faces, however, are similar to communities with hazardous waste sites and other environmental hazards and therefore should be considered in this discussion. In July 1994 and March 1998, tropical storms unleashed unprecedented amounts of rain over southwest Georgia, creating the worst flooding in Georgia's history. Although a large portion of the state from metropolitan Atlanta to the Georgia-Florida border was affected, south Albany's black, low-income communities suffered the greatest damage and faced the most challenging recovery.

Community residents began organizing as they waited in the Federal Emergency Management Agency lines. At first, attention was focused on the cause of the damage, which was disproportionately concentrated in black neighborhoods and business districts. Allegations were made that the flood gates had been intentionally manipulated to prevent flooding in more affluent, white areas. Some residents were also concerned that many residents would not return to build a viable community. The flood left victims with many questions involving the health impact of the disaster, protection against fraud, and the resources that would be made available to rebuild their communities.

To respond to the residents' needs and to advocate on the community's behalf, the South Side Mega Flood Task Force was formed. It is the only grassroots organization presently working in the community. The short-term objective is to find solutions for any flood-related problem or concern that arises. The long-term objective is to have residents create and implement a plan for rebuilding their neighborhoods. The organization has employed various strategies to meet the many concerns and needs of flood victims. For example, the possible flood gate manipulation was interpreted as an issue of social justice. The Reverend Jesse Jackson, civil rights leader, brought national exposure to the community's struggle. Hundreds of citizens attended meetings to discuss the allegations. A public hearing for flood victims and a march of 200 people increased the community's awareness and brought further visibility to the issue. To satisfy the demands of the activists, the Georgia Environmental Protection Division launched an investigation into the claim and concluded that nothing had been done to worsen the impact of the flood on the black community. Residents, however, still have questions about the unusual flooding in their area, and interest in legal action remains.

Another problem faced by the task force is the possibility of increased health risks resulting from the flood and the substandard living conditions left by the disaster. Although residents were told that no health problems resulted from the disaster, the task force began compiling their own list of cases and gathering data. For example, the group discovered that a landfill had been ruptured by the flooding, creating a public health and environmental hazard. Community residents photographed the site to document the problem. These tactics provided them with the concrete evidence they needed to confront city officials with their concerns.

One of the greatest achievements of the group to date is the establishment of a funded center where residents can receive personal help with flood-related problems. According to the founder of the task force, many residents are not able to negotiate the procedures for getting assistance. The center will assist individuals with any problem, from filling out applications to informing people about the services that are available. To meet long-term recovery goals, the center helps organize neighborhoods into block groups that will plan the reconstruction of their respective communities. The center will expedite the implementation of neighborhood plans by interfacing with government agencies and nongovernmental organizations that have the needed resources.

Although the task force has not entered into formal coalitions with other organizations, the creation of partnerships with government agencies and voluntary organizations is essential in responding to the wide range of needs encountered at the center. Because it is not feasible to house all the services within the center, the group has created a network of resources by establishing relationships with other groups and agencies. For example, Georgia Legal Services is working with the task force to educate residents about their rights. The Better Business Bureau is offering seminars and preparing materials to help the task force address the community's concerns about fraud. The Senior Citizens Garden Club is assisting with landscaping damaged areas. In addition, to learn from the experiences of other communities, the task force plans to network with similar grassroots groups that have formed in Miami and Charleston.

The task force does not perceive itself as primarily an environmental group. Instead, the group takes a holistic approach to the community's problems and focuses on environmental issues when they arise. The founder of the task force, however, does feel that an environmental justice framework has been employed in the community's response to a devastating natural disaster (M. Young-Cummings, personal communication, September 11, 1995).

A Second Major Flood in Albany, Georgia

The road to reconstruction and recovery has been a long and arduous one for the black Albany community devastated by flooding in 1994. Since the floods, the South Side Mega Flood Task Force worked to organize neighborhoods into block groups that would work directly with the city and others to plan the reconstruction of the community. According to the organization's founder, representatives of block groups came to a number of meetings to provide input; the process, however, has been too slow. Houses and other structures still sit abandoned and damaged by flood waters. The task force has begun to look at alternative strategies to rebuild the community and is considering becoming a community development corporation that would buy damaged structures, provide jobs to community members to rebuild them, and then provide structures for low-cost housing and other community needs.

While in the midst of carrying out its work in long-term reconstruction and recovery, the task force and the community experienced two more natural disasters that tested their level of disaster preparedness and their ability to provide disaster relief in an already hurting community. In 1995, a tornado damaged more than 200 houses in Albany, many of which were in the black community. The American Red Cross immediately set up a service center; the center was located, however, several miles away from the area suffering the most damage. Survivors were reluctant to go to the center because they did not want to leave their belongings unprotected. Several days later, the South Side Mega

Flood Task Force was asked and agreed to host the ARC service center, which moved to within three blocks of the damaged area. The resulting collaboration between the ARC, the task force, and other local groups was a model of efficient disaster relief. The federally funded Job Corps created a cooking and dining area at the center and brought enough food to feed approximately 100 people every day. The American Federation of State, County, and Municipal Employees Union also provided donations and assistance such as cooking, child care, and cleanup for damaged structures. Many community residents also donated time and items needed by the affected families. An indication of the success of this partnership is the ability of the ARC to contact and provide services to all the survivors in half the time that was allotted for the service center to complete its work.

In March of 1998, a second flooding occurred in Albany. Although flooding almost as severe as the 1994 flooding was forecast, the actual amount of water and therefore damage was significantly less. According to the task force founder, the community was better prepared in 1998, but, more important, the governmental agencies responsible for disaster response handled the threat differently the second time. For example, the warnings came much earlier, structures were sandbagged, and hundreds of people were evacuated for about 1 week from their homes. This time, the damage not only was less but also was more evenly distributed throughout the affluent and poor, and black and white, areas of town.

Although the high level of response and the outcome of the 1998 flooding suggest that the presence of a community-based and created group has been able to bring the concerns of the south Albany community into the dialogue of how disasters are handled and mitigated, other events testify to the difficulty of sustaining partnerships between residents and governmental and nongovernmental agencies with resources, particularly when the organizations representing the voice of the community become dependent on government or foundation funding to build their community visions. Shortly before the 1998 flooding, the South Side Mega Flood Task Force experienced a financial setback and consequently was unable to respond to the floods. Their long-term work for reconstruction from the earlier floods is also in jeopardy, and the organization's future is uncertain.

THE ENVIRONMENTAL JUSTICE FRAMEWORK

Although every response to an environmental hazard is unique to that community and setting, a general description of how African Americans have coped with environmental threats to health can be generated from the case studies presented in this chapter and the numerous other examples in the literature. Specifically, we can look at the organization of communities, the strategies employed, and the role of coalitions and partnerships that characterize the environmental justice framework.

1. *The environmental hazard is perceived within a larger context of civil rights and human justice.*

Perhaps the greatest difference between mainstream environmentalists and the environmental justice groups is in the perception of the problem (Taylor, 1993). People of color have not argued for the preservation of nature at the expense of human well-being. Nor have they simply opposed the environmental hazard in their community (the NIMBY approach). Instead, they question why they are asked to bear so much of the burden of these hazards without receiving an equal share of the benefits. Black environmentalists ask why the agencies charged with protecting people's health and the quality of the environment are failing to apply their protective measures and policies uniformly. Environmental protection and hazard distribution have been linked to civil rights, human justice, and survival. Therefore, the solutions address not only the immediate problem posed by the hazard but also the right of all human beings to live in healthy environments and have equal protection under the law.

To residents in afflicted communities, bearing the burden of an unwanted facility without sharing in the benefits is a violation of human rights. This was the perception of southwest Atlantans who questioned why they should treat the entire region's wastewater while the other communities enjoyed a better quality of life. A frequently perceived benefit is industry's promise of new jobs. Economic trade-off has often been used as a means to justify the establishment of undesirable facilities in impoverished areas. Black residents often find that many of the promised jobs are given to people from outside the community or conclude that pro-growth attitudes and policies have led to exploitation (Bullard, 1992).

Environmental racism is a key concept that defines environmental issues as questions of civil rights and social justice. Racism can influence the distribution of hazards and protection in numerous ways. Although the claim of racism may be obvious, as in the flood allegations in Albany, more covert forms of institutional racism are often to blame. For example, racially segregated housing patterns prevent many African Americans, regardless of income level, from moving away from unwanted land use facilities. Environmental policies reflect the dominant power structures in society, which are racially biased. The application of such policies and the enforcement of regulations are also affected by race, as demonstrated by the *National Law Journal*'s study (Lavelle & Coyle,

1992). Racism, in its many forms, plays an important part in the environmental justice framework.

2. *Leadership and membership may be composed not of environmentalists but rather of a group of social and community activists who come together to work on environmental issues.*

This trend was observed by Bullard (1994a) in his study of four African American communities. Few community residents belonged to environmental organizations. Residents did belong to many voluntary associations, however, which provided a membership base for the communities' efforts. Of the household heads, 76% were members of the black church, a historically active institution. Community improvement and parent groups also accounted for much of the membership in voluntary organizations. This lack of reliance on environmental organizations for leadership and support is a key distinction between the emerging black environmentalism and mainstream environmentalism.

In the communities described in this chapter, group leadership and membership were also initiated from nonenvironmental organizations. Instead, churches, neighborhood, and political activist groups took the lead in challenging environmental issues. The groups in Albany and Atlanta took holistic approaches to addressing problems in their community and adopted environmental foci when the need arose.

Other case studies described in the literature demonstrate this pattern. For example, a parents' association in Harlem, New York City, took the lead in investigating asbestos in the children's school (Freudenberg, 1984). School authorities were aware of the asbestos but did nothing to correct the problem. In response, the parents' association hired a laboratory to conduct tests and succeeded in closing down the school for 7 months until asbestos removal could be completed. These examples point to a pattern of membership recruitment in African American communities facing environmental threats. In the historical absence of strong environmental organizations in communities of color, black environmentalism as observed by Bullard (1994a) has emerged from "the pre-existing social structures and institutions within the racially-segregated and politically-oppressed black community" (p. 95).

3. *Strategies employed generally include education and consciousness raising, legal and legislative action, and direct action.*

Within the environmental justice framework, many strategies can be employed, depending on the context and resources available to the group. Educating community members about the various dimensions of the issue is frequently the first step to launching an effective campaign against an environmental threat. Lack of information may be the first hurdle to overcome, so residents can effectively communicate with the government officials or corporation representatives that hold the balance of power. For example, the residents of southwest Atlanta were told that the sewage treatment system was too technical and complicated for laypersons to understand, and that therefore the residents should trust the city to make the appropriate decisions. In response, residents spent a great deal of time trying to learn about the issue so that they could begin to voice a community perspective and participate in the planning process. In this case, networking and coalitions were useful tools for providing a source of information on an issue with which the community had little prior experience. Other successful educational campaigns have been built using community forums, public speaking, and mass media (Freudenberg, 1984). In Albany and Atlanta, residents held meetings to discuss the environmental hazard. Members of JPAP frequently go to conferences and other communities to make presentations about their efforts. Mass media were used by Atlanta residents, who arranged press conferences at locations where sewage could be seen running through streets or yards.

Residents may also be required to provide documentation of the impact of a given hazard. The information may not be known or freely shared with the residents. In response, many environmental justice groups have conducted their own surveys to uncover the health risks in a community. JPAP and the South Side Mega Flood Task Force have used such methods. Another community affected by elevated blood lead levels in children found that the results of a screening conducted by the state would not be shared with the children's parents (Phoenix, 1993). Therefore, the community conducted its own minority health survey in eight languages. Other forms of documentation have included hiring researchers to conduct investigations, photographing health hazards, and mapping the pathways of pollution (e.g., walking sewer lines to identify cracks in the system).

Political strategies are used to influence policies regarding exposure to the hazard, hold corporations and the government accountable for their actions, and gain electoral support (Freudenberg, 1984). In the three cases presented in this chapter, political strategies increased community residents' control over decision making, resource allocation, and community development planning. For many years, African Americans have struggled to assert their voice in political processes; therefore, it is a logical focus for environmental justice groups. Such an approach often requires a coordinated effort to have consistent community representation at committee meetings and wide representation at public hearings. The media are also a tool that has been used to publicize injustices. All these strategies were employed by residents in southwest Atlanta, whose efforts culminated in a victory at the city council.

Legal action is also an appealing strategy. Lawsuits have succeeded in stopping some environmental hazards, such as the use of the pesticide DDT, and they have increased public awareness of certain issues (Freudenberg, 1984). Legal strategies, however, require time and money. In addition, residents may become frustrated with the difficulty in obtaining an unbiased hearing. For example, in Texarkana (in Texas and Arkansas), residents were plagued by three hazardous waste sites, a controversial landfill, and industrial polluters (Capek, 1993). Initially, 58 families came together to sue one of the polluting companies but became disillusioned by their defeat. Their trust in the legal system was further undermined by their experiences with EPA. Their dissatisfaction with legal strategies eventually led them to pursue direct action methods.

Direct action strategies, employed by civil rights and social activists, are strongly suggested by the environmental justice framework. This approach was first demonstrated by hundreds of Warren County protesters who lay in the street in an attempt to prevent trucks carrying PCB-contaminated soil into a landfill. Members of the Texarkana group, like many other environmental justice groups, used marches, press conferences, direct encounters with officials, and letter-writing campaigns to reach their goals (Capek, 1993). Citing a number of successes resulting from direct confrontational tactics, Freudenberg (1984) argues that direct action through community organizing is the most effective tool for environmentalists.

Community groups generally employ multiple strategies to achieve their objectives. Some groups have been successful, whereas others have suffered numerous frustrations and setbacks. Ultimately, regardless of outcomes, the environmental justice framework is a process that empowers people of color, allowing them to participate more fully in the political process and to gain control over the environmental hazards that affect their health.

4. *Coalition building and partnerships enable communities to gain access to power, experience, and resources to confront environmental hazards.*

Taylor (1992) lists three options available to address concerns when African Americans are faced with an environmental threat: join an existing environmental group, form a new group to fight the issue without outside help, and form a new group that is linked to others through coalitions and networks. She concludes that the third option, coalition and network building, seems to work best for newly formed groups.

For many environmental justice groups, coalition or partnership building has been an effective way to increase access to resources, skills, and political strength and to learn from the experience of others. Whether the group has joined formal coalitions such as JPAP, loose confederations such as the neighborhood planning unit in Atlanta, or a network of partnerships such as Albany, the group can benefit from the relationships. In small communities such as Columbia, coalitions are a way of obtaining access to resources and information that are unavailable within the community. In other cases such as Atlanta, resources available within the city were not fully used during the early stages of community opposition. The creation of networks based on common goals has enabled the residents in the Atlanta neighborhood to draw support and assistance from groups throughout the city.

Coalitions link resources and expertise at many levels. Partnerships may be forged between nonenvironmental organizations and environmental groups, grassroots groups and government agencies, and local groups and regional and national organizations. The establishment of national clearinghouses, public information services, and regional networks, such as the Southeast Organizing Committee, have facilitated the formation of umbrella organizations and coalitions. Notable conferences including the Urban Environmental Health Conference, the Race and the Incidence of Environmental Hazards Conference, and the first National People of Color Environmental Leadership Conference have further encouraged the collaboration of groups to form the environmental justice movement (Lee, 1993).

Organizing efforts led by African Americans have been able to generate broad support from various segments of a community, creating interracial and interclass collaborative efforts. Such was the case in Halifax County, Virginia, where black and white community leaders and residents joined to fight a decision to establish a storage facility for nuclear waste in a low-income, black section of the county (Collin & Harris, 1993). Observers have noted the benefit to mainstream environmental groups of mobilizing the support of black environmental and civil rights activists, including increased community support and broader definition of issues (Freudenberg, 1984). Advocates of increased cooperation between environmental justice and mainstream groups believe that coalitions have been effective and mutually beneficial. Although mainstream organizations contribute technical, legal, and lobbying experience, environmental justice groups have expertise in community organizing and social justice (Adams, 1992).

Coalitions, however, have not always succeeded in bridging the gaps between organizations sharing a common concern. A case in point is Sumter County, Alabama (Bailey, Faupel, & Gundlach, 1993). Sumter County has a long history of racial segregation and white dominance of economic and political power. It is also home to the "Cadillac" of hazardous waste landfills, the largest in the nation. The black community, through an organization called the Minority People's Council, led the early opposition to the landfill.

Most of the opposition, however, has come from a small, white, radical group, Alabamians for a Clean Environment, that splintered off from a more conservative, white environmental group. According to Bailey et al. (1993), a tentative alliance has formed between black civil rights activists and the white environmentalists, but a successful alliance has yet to be established. Bailey et al. attribute this largely to the white environmentalists' narrow focus on one issue and failure to address the broader social, economic, and political issues of concern to the black community. Although coalition building is not always a smooth process, careful consideration of coalition partners may help prevent the barriers encountered in Sumter County. Freudenberg (1984) lists several questions to guide the building of effective coalitions:

> When environmental activists look for partners in their campaigns against exposure to toxic chemicals or other hazards, they ask several questions about their potential allies. How strong are they? What experience or skills do they have to offer? What is their stake in the status quo? How can they help to increase the movement's political power? (p. 210)

Despite difficulties inherent in collaborating with diverse groups, coalition building and network and partnership development appear to be valuable strategies. As noted earlier, African Americans and other people of color are disproportionately affected by environmental hazards, including air and water pollution, hazardous waste disposal, lead poisoning, and natural disasters. Environmental health, therefore, is a serious health issue for the black community. And it has not been ignored, as many people have tried to maintain. History and research demonstrate that African Americans throughout the country have taken, and continue to take, a proactive approach to restoring and protecting environmental health. For the most part, this health promotion activity has taken the shape of the environmental justice movement.

Numerous case studies have documented the effectiveness of the environmental justice movement in addressing environmental risks to communities of color. The framework incorporates a variety of strategies to correct injustices and inequities in environmental hazard distribution and protection. Community organizing and coalition and partnership building that bring together resources and create group solidarity in politically disenfranchised communities are essential to this process. Given the growing strength of the environmental justice movement and the record of past successes, this framework can be considered an effective means of improving the health and the quality of life of African Americans threatened by environmental hazards.

7

Rural Coalitions and Substance Abuse Prevention
A Case Study Approach

This chapter focuses on the development and functioning of 10 rural coalitions in the state of Georgia. The 10 coalitions were sponsored by the U.S. Center for Substance Abuse Prevention and constitute the primary basis for the discussion presented on rural coalitions. Consistent with the mission of the center, the coalitions' primary goal was the prevention of drug abuse among a specifically identified target group.

In the identification of resources for the development of this chapter, we compiled data from a group of coalitions that constituted a larger program called Project RECLAIM (Rural/Empowered Coalitions for Long-Range Approaches to Inside Management). These coalitions, geographically located in 10 counties, functioned during a 3-year period as Project RECLAIM, although some of the groups continued independently of Project RECLAIM after the program end date. In an examination of these coalitions that existed in 10 areas encompassing rural parts of Georgia, this chapter presents a case study approach toward an enhanced understanding of the work of coalitions in rural areas. Table 7.1 shows these counties with selected demographic information including total population, median income, and number of physicians for selected years. (Figures are for the entire county as opposed to the specific area of the county hosting a particular coalition.)

The development of coalitions in rural areas is beset with a special set of challenges. In many rural settings, primary health care is often provided by nurse practitioners and physician assistants with supervision of physicians who

TABLE 7.1 Demographics by County

County	1990 Population	1989 Total Median Income	1989 Black Median Income	Total/Black Percentage Completed High School	1996 Number of Practicing Physicians
Bartow	55,911	26,312	22,418	34.4/31.5	54
Hall	95,428	27,397	18,800	30.0/32.4	219
Hancock	8,908	15,377	15,101	34.1/32.9	7
Lowndes	75,981	22,309	13,684	31.7/28.5	139
McDuffie	20,119	20,322	13,702	30.7/26.2	15
Muscogee	179,278	22,716	16,286	29.9/29.9	409
Peach	21,189	23,642	14,001	31.0/21.6	11
Richmond	189,719	23,497	18,500	30.1/28.7	1193
Toombs	24,072	18,897	11,084	31.7/28.0	32
Washington	19,112	19,365	13,676	36.5/32.5	16

SOURCE: Bachtel & Boatright (1991).

may be located a considerable distance away. Generally, primary care professionals are scarce in rural areas. Family practice physicians and midlevel practitioners are often seen in the provision of primary care services. Not only are rural residents faced with a disadvantaged situation relative to the particular issue of health care personnel, but also other specific problems exist that contrast to those in more densely populated areas.

Residents of rural communities tend to have a lower degree of life chances than their urban counterparts. Overall, they are poorer, sicker, and more likely to be uninsured (Rowland & Lyons, 1989). Given that persons living in rural communities tend to lag behind urban residents on key health status indicators, and in light of the foregoing chapters' discussion of coalition formation, it seems that the rural environment is a most appropriate one for the development of coalitions. In half of the 10 coalitions studied for this chapter, previous alliances for health promotion had existed, including those that targeted heart, lung, and cancer awareness. Because death rates tend to be higher in rural areas (especially for certain conditions), it follows that strategies such as coalitions designed to combat the situation are becoming increasingly popular in these areas. Table 7.2 depicts the leading causes of death in 1989 for the counties included in this discussion.

COALITION COMPOSITION

By requirement of the funding agency (the Center for Substance Abuse Prevention), the 10 rural coalitions each consisted of a minimum of seven partners.

TABLE 7.2 Leading Causes of Death: 1989 (in number/percentages)

County	Cancer	Heart Attack	Stroke	Respiratory Diseases	Injuries & Poisoning	Deaths From All Other Causes
Bartow	124/20.9	105/17.7	39/6.6	61/10.3	44/7.4	114/19.2
Hall	181/19.9	176/19.3	86/9.4	94/10.3	73/8.0	203/22.3
Hancock	19/17.4	12/11.0	9/8.3	5/4.6	16/14.7	18/16.5
Lowndes	146/22.2	90/13.7	50/7.6	60/9.1	45/6.8	142/21.5
McDuffie	41/17.4	32/13.6	20/8.5	26/11.1	18/7.7	76/32.3
Muscogee	364/20.9	321/18.4	110/6.3	181/10.4	90/5.2	397/22.8
Peach	35/20.1	31/17.8	9/5.2	15/8.6	15/8.6	45.25.9
Richmond	388/20.0	351/18.1	130/6.7	182/9.4	144/7.4	378/19.5
Toombs	61/23.5	13/5.0	21/8.1	34/13.1	28/10.8	39/15.0
Washington	45/20.9	29/13.5	23/10.7	21/9.8	10/4.7	58/27.0

SOURCE: Bachtel & Boatright (1991).

The various partners included representatives from the media, religious community, social services, schools/education, law enforcement, government, and private industry. Although each of the 10 coalitions had partnerships that differed in the number of members as well as organizations and agencies represented, each was sufficiently represented to maintain a viable coalition. Each coalition was defined by a unique set of partners and sought to be representative of the respective community. In meeting these and other criteria, Project RECLAIM was categorically positioned to be successful in reaching major objectives. Its inclusion of a diverse set of partners provided an advantage from the outset.

To better ensure that the concerns of all community residents are met, coalitions should strive toward diversity. This entails inclusion of both men and women and persons of different ethnicities. The data in Table 7.3 show coalition composition by race and gender and the number of partners per coalition.

Recruitment and Retention of Partners

To successfully maintain a coalition in rural communities, the coalition's objectives and goals must be important to community residents. Our experiences clearly indicate that plans for a community coalition need to be drafted by that particular community. No matter how well programs have worked for similar coalitions, void of direct input and development by the coalition members themselves, the work takes on a tenuous start.

During the formative stages of the 10 coalitions examined for this study, residents of each coalition were invited to discuss the community issues that

TABLE 7.3 Coalition Representation by Race and Gender

County	Total Number Partners	Number/% Black Partners	Number/% Women Partners
Hall	14	9/64	6/43
Washington	15	10/67	8/53
Toombs	10	5/50	3/30
Richmond	20	17/85	12/60
Muscogee	8	6/75	2/25
McDuffie	20	8/40	10/50
Peach	14	8/57	8/57
Lowndes	10	5/50	4/40
Hancock	16	13/81	5/31
Bartow	20	11/55	8/40

were most important to them and their families. On the basis of concerns of the communities (identified through a survey research process), coalition members drafted objectives emanating from this input.

Stakeholders and Coalition Survival

The coalitions were charged by the funding agency with assuming responsibility for actively promoting improved health. This included the promotion of drug-free behaviors among community residents. On the basis of an empowerment model, residents were introduced to a plan designed to put them in control of their own destinies (Braithwaite, 1992). Through a commitment to active participation in decision making and to addressing policy issues that affect their quality of life, residents were encouraged to become vested stakeholders.

Becoming a stakeholder holds privileges and responsibilities. According to Project RECLAIM coalition members, although privileges associated with belonging to a coalition can be incredible (especially when coalition objectives are met), the responsibilities can be even more incredible. In the context of coalition work and black women's activism, Reagon (1983) discusses the energies expended in doing coalition work. Although her cause is much broader than that of many of the coalitions described in this book, the points made can still be applied. Anyone who has played an integral role in coalition development can attest to the intense labor involved. Her description of the harshness of coalition work is captured in the following:

I feel as if I'm gonna keel over any minute and die. That is often what it feels like if you're *really* doing coalition work. Most of the time you feel threatened to the core and if you don't, you're not really doing no coalescing. (p. 356)

Although the extent to which pain is felt by a coalition member varies with a number of factors (including the nature of the overall goal), many of the members in the 10 counties examined attested to a distinct degree of labor associated with their work. A common issue was the unintended time spent to cover unexpected problems and gaps left by "noncommitted" members. One coalition member confided that more time was spent on the partnership than on her regular job.

Reagon (1983) jovially warns about letting the coalition interfere unnecessarily. Her advice is to know how to pull back. She states, "A coalition *can* kill people; however, it is not by nature fatal. You do not have to die because you are committed to a coalition" (p. 361).

Although there are major differences between the substance of Reagon's cause in this particular instance and that of Project RECLAIM, her message makes a clear point about the work necessary for coalition success. The case of Project RECLAIM shows, however, that there is an apparent relationship between being a vested stakeholder and the degree of effort expended. Although it was expected that the more committed members would expend more time on coalition activities, we found in addition that these individuals were less likely to construe their experiences as "laborious" or in otherwise adverse terms. Hence, it appears that the survival of coalition work, at least for a group of rural partners, is related to having a perspective. The perspective takes into account the pros and cons of coalition building and weighs them in the context of the larger picture.

RURAL AMERICA IN REVIEW

According to the 1990 census, almost 4 million (3,832,616) African Americans resided in rural areas, compared with virtually 26 million (26,153,444) who lived in urban areas (U.S. Bureau of the Census, 1992). Approximately 25% of all Americans live in rural areas; approximately 33% of all African Americans live in rural areas. Of the nation's poor, 38% reside in rural areas. Moreover, of 86 counties nationwide in which one third or more of the population is in poverty, all but one are nonmetropolitan in nature (Joint Task Force of the National Association of Community Health Centers and the National Rural Health Association [Joint Task Force], 1989).

Poverty among rural residents has its costs. Those living in rural areas are more likely to suffer from chronic disease conditions including arthritis, visual and hearing impairments, ulcers, thyroid and kidney problems, heart disease, hypertension, and emphysema. They are also more likely to suffer limitations in activity as a result of chronic conditions in comparison with their urban counterparts (Joint Task Force, 1989).

Problems related to health care for rural residents go beyond a higher prevalence of chronic health conditions for these Americans. Compounding this bleak picture is the lack of health insurance for an appreciable number of rural Americans. All rural residents, as a group, have a 15% higher rate of uninsuredness than the U.S. average and a 24% higher rate than their metropolitan counterparts. Rural residents pay on average 10% more of their income out-of-pocket for health care than do their urban counterparts. For impoverished rural communities, the additional drain of out-of-pocket costs for health care presents a significant problem. Among the poor, those supposedly protected by the "safety net," rural residents experience a 10% higher rate of uninsuredness than the U.S. average, and a 44% higher rate than their metropolitan counterparts (Joint Task Force, 1989).

Problems for rural residents relative to health care also include the shortage of doctors and nurses. The plight of a shortage of health care personnel haunts many rural areas. For the 10 counties included in this study, a majority could identify with this problem. Table 7.4 shows the number of physicians by specialty for each county.

Other problems include the allocation of public monies, especially at the federal level. For example, although one fourth of all Americans live in rural areas, public funding for health care in rural America has consistently lagged behind the U.S. average. Nationally, per capita expenditures for health and related services are far lower for rural residents: 42% fewer health service dollars per capita than the U.S. average and 50% fewer social service dollars per capita than the U.S. average. Programs with combined federal and state responsibility also show this disparity: 70% of the rural poor live in states in which the maximum AFDC benefits are below the national median. In addition, the rate of qualification for public assistance is 37% lower in rural areas, and more than 75% of the rural poor do not qualify for public assistance (Joint Task Force, 1989). These statistics, combined with the aforementioned problems of health care personnel shortage and a void in adequate insurance, portend a dismal outlook for rural residents. Issues of unemployment and underemployment as well as those surrounding the closing of hospitals and the loss of farmland further compound the picture.

In rural Georgia, hospitals and other health care centers are experiencing an especially grave situation in their struggle to survive. These facilities are being forced to close or consolidate in the face of managed care. A shortage of physicians exists in many rural areas, and hospitals in these same areas are underused. For example, one such hospital located in Louisville, Georgia, attempts to stay afloat despite an occupancy rate of less than 15%. This and

TABLE 7.4 Number of Physicians by Specialty: 1990

County	Family Practice	OB/GYN	Pediatrics	Internal Medicine	General Surgery	Other	Total	Total Rate per 100,000 Population
Bartow	13	6	3	5	2	25	54	83.0
Hall	27	16	13	20	14	129	219	198.8
Hancock	4	2	0	1	0	0	7	76.0
Lowndes	19	9	6	11	9	85	139	168.3
McDuffie	4	0	0	6	2	3	15	68.6
Muscogee	96	16	19	34	16	228	409	215.4
Peach	8	0	0	2	0	1	11	49.2
Richmond	92	76	81	147	57	740	1193	588.0
Toombs	7	3	2	8	2	10	32	125.3
Washington	5	1	1	4	3	2	16	79.6

SOURCE: Bachtel & Boatright (1991).

similar rates across certain Georgia hospitals portend a serious crisis for rural health care. Hospital closures in small communities that have typically been used by poor residents pose a gap in health care for this population. In the absence of these hospitals and clinics where doors are being forced closed, community residents' access to alternative health care centers can be severely limited.

STRATEGIES AND CHALLENGES IN RURAL COMMUNITIES

In an effort to reduce the difficulties faced by rural residents' access to health care, some strategies have become prominent. The past couple of decades have ushered in much interest in coalitions, partnerships, alliances, or some other term used to describe the pooling of resources for the promotion of a common goal. Particularly for African American and other historically depressed ethnic groups, the development of coalitions appears to be a promising strategy.

Much has been written about the importance of pooling resources toward the enhancement of communities. Merging various resources, whether financial or some other form (e.g., personnel), carries certain benefits. The combining of resources is especially consequential for rural populations. In the organizing of coalitions for health promotion in rural areas, attention must be directed toward a special set of challenges. Included among these are the logistics involved in the planning and execution of program strategies. Because rural communities tend to be less developed than those in urban areas, a special set of problems can occur in the strategizing for community development.

The 10 counties examined in this study all indicated varying degrees of strength relative to a set of conditions typically seen as important to the success of coalitions. (See the list of conditions delineated as areas of needed training in the appendix. We identified these 32 areas on the basis of our experiences with coalition development.) Regardless of a particular need, the acknowledgment and willingness to fill the void are important to the coalition's progress.

During the developmental stages of the coalitions, the 10 counties studied indicated that their greatest needs included community mobilization strategies and general development with substance abuse prevention programs. The problems that beset coalitions during the formative stages often are associated with acceptable representation and issues of turf. On the basis of the experiences of the rural counties in Georgia, it is safe to say that a common set of challenges tended to confront the various coalitions. Despite the surfacing of several specific areas as problematic for a given county, certain challenges were found to be common among the coalitions. For example, the data bear out that friction associated with turf was apparent in each of the 10 coalitions.

Community mobilization strategies were identified as most important by a majority of the coalitions. This points to the importance of a clear guide to getting coalitions off to a start that leads to success. Other important areas for development include assistance in the development and execution of substance abuse prevention programs and the selection and development of health interventions. Table 7.5 depicts the needs identified most often by the coalitions and the number of coalitions that identified a particular area as *high need*. For a listing of all needs, see the appendix.

CHARACTERISTICS OF A WELL-FUNCTIONING RURAL COALITION

All the coalitions except one indicated that training in drug prevention program development was necessary for their growth. Five coalitions identified a need for training in community mobilization strategies. Four coalitions cited health intervention selection and development. IRS tax-exempt status and long-range planning were targeted by three coalitions each. All other areas of need listed in the appendix were deemed necessary by two or fewer coalitions.

Although the 10 rural coalitions studied all had strengths to varying degrees, there was one in particular that progressed exceptionally well. This coalition, located in Bartow County, tended to lead the other groups in a number of categories, including meeting attendance and general follow-through. The Bartow County Coalition epitomized several of the guidelines generally accepted

TABLE 7.5 Most Commonly Identified Training Needs: Project RECLAIM

Training Area	Number of Counties With Need
Drug prevention program development	9
Community mobilization strategies	5
Health intervention selection/development	4
IRS tax-exempt status	3
Long-range planning	3

for the development and sustaining of coalitions. First, this coalition was headed by a person who had committed substantial time and energy to the partnership. This individual served not only as one of the distinct leaders of the coalition but also as a prominent leader in the community. Although some turnover was characteristic of some of the other coalitions, the Bartow County Coalition maintained this constant leader throughout the entire period of its federal funding. The coalition leader was highly motivated by the mission of the coalition, and the enthusiasm exhibited carried over to other coalition members. Overall, the presence of strong leadership skills promoted the completion of tasks and follow-through with respect to other activities of the coalition.

Second, the Bartow County Coalition also possessed a collective commitment to the objectives and ultimate goal. The capacity of this coalition to be relatively united (especially in comparison with the other nine coalitions studied) expressed the degree of unity necessary for a successful coalition. Because the coalition was united in its goal and the ways to reach this goal, disputes were minimized, and the work of the group could be better facilitated.

In many other ways, albeit more esoteric than those typically discussed as important to a successful coalition (for example, participation in planned programs sponsored by the coalition), the Bartow County Coalition cooperatively carried out its stated duties. When challenges beset its group, designated leaders and other executive board members tended to attribute such to the lack of funds. Although all 10 coalitions were awarded funds to carry out their respective objectives related to substance abuse prevention, these funds were sometimes inaccessible because of logistical problems. According to key officers of the Bartow County Coalition, the inability to access funds in a timely matter blocked a number of initiatives from being completed as scheduled. For example, in a discussion of the problem, the president related, "We keep trying to be self-sufficient, and when we try, they throw in a blocker."

Unfortunately, the difficulties surrounding monies did not occur as isolated events. Receiving expected funds in a timely manner constituted a problem on several occasions. In a different interview with the coalition's president, a similar sentiment was relayed.

> We were told that we would get funding at the start of the new funding cycle but now we have been informed that this will be delayed. . . . How do they expect us to function on our own when they keep changing the direction?

These comments illustrate another criterion for a successful coalition: an adequate operating budget. In the absence of sufficient funding for a coalition's duties, the coalition is doomed from the beginning. Several authors have discussed the role of finances and its importance to a coalition's functioning (McLaughlin, Zellers, & Brown, 1989; Stern, 1991).

Some authors have offered ideas about developing coalitions that are relevant to the experiences of the partnerships studied in this chapter. From our examination of the 10 coalitions' activities and overall efforts, we can say that those beset with the least problems were the ones more closely aligned with the following characteristics.

1. *Strong leadership:* The importance of a strong head (whether designated as coordinator, chair, president, etc.) represents an obvious characteristic. Too often, the efforts of a coalition are only as effective as that group's leader. The group's leader has the responsibility of articulating the objectives and goals of the coalition, providing sustained motivation so that member involvement is constant, and juggling competing interests among other tasks. An ineffective leader places an unnecessary burden on the coalition to make up for his or her inadequacies. Often, a coalition is unable to rebound from a bad leader despite strong efforts on its own to execute the coalition's mission. One of the 10 coalitions studied had a particular challenge with the lack of strong leadership. The president of this coalition was often absent from meetings and largely detached from the operations and business of the group. The coalition functioned to a large extent from the input of other officers and executive board members who attempted to fill voids as needed. Because of issues of authority and procedure, however, the work of these subordinate officers was limited.

2. *Representative input:* Representation from all factions of the community is important to the coalition's successful functioning. Some typical components of coalitions within black rural areas include the church, education, government (health and human service agencies), law enforcement, and, of course, the community (grassroots representation). Not only is it important for representation to occur, but also it is equally important that the various components actively work together in a collegial manner. Because representatives of these areas are often those who constitute the executive board, it is also important

that coalitions attempt to seek out influential or top-level members. Hence, representation ideally should be broad and also include members who hold some authority within the capacity represented. The support of the coalition from top- or executive-level members provides a degree of legitimacy to the coalition that often serves as validation for potential influential members.

3. *Commitment to a common goal:* One of the necessary ingredients in a health care coalition is a shared interest in a particular problem and a shared commitment to solving it (Gottlieb, Brink, & Gingiss, 1993). The success of a coalition, especially one dependent on a relatively small cadre of members, as often is the case in rural black areas, rests with full embracement of the cause by each member. In the absence of a strong commitment to the coalition's goal(s), the partnership is destined to fall short of its ultimate goal. Not only does the reaching of goals become elusive, but more fundamental, sheer efforts toward objectives take on a piecemeal slant.

4. *Access to adequate funds:* For a coalition to implement activities leading to its goals, an operating budget is required. Although discussions and planning meetings may not require funds, a budget is necessary if action is to ensue from these deliberations. In the case of the 10 coalitions examined here, funding was provided by the Center for Substance Abuse Prevention. Given the importance of a basic operating budget for any worthwhile endeavor, it should be clear why funds would be needed to proceed with the work of the 10 coalitions. In the particular case of black rural areas, a budget is often necessary for incentives specifically targeted toward participation, including getting individuals to meetings. These incentives can take the form of prizes (cash or otherwise) and/or light food or refreshments.

Work Groups

Coalitions depend heavily on the hours committed by the respective coalition partners. If all partners that constitute a part of the coalition do their fair share, goals and objectives can be more easily met. Because the different partners that composed the 10 rural coalitions in this study represented a diverse set of players, there appeared to be more opportunity for promoting the coalition's cause (as previously discussed). Coalitions having a mixed or diverse member-ship (as opposed to partners from one or two organizations exclusively) tend to wield a stronger political agenda. Although mixed-base coalitions can be difficult to manage (in part because their memberships often struggle with both the ends and means of the coalitions), a diverse membership should be the goal in coalition development. The disadvantages associated with having a diverse set of members within a coalition can be offset by the resources offered by the combined group. Moreover, simply because a coalition is composed of a narrow set of partners or members, ease of management is not necessarily ensured. An analysis of the monthly reports on the development of the 10 coalitions studied shows that some of the greatest friction came from those coalitions that were composed of fewer diverse partners. The coalitions that led the way in cordial meetings and effective teamwork included at least two that were the most diverse of all the 10 studied.

These successful coalitions were characterized by a focused agenda and tended to be the most task oriented of the groups. Dluhy (1990) states that "the heart of the successful coalition is the work group" (p. 54). Work groups or special committees are goal oriented and are responsible for executing coalition tasks. Because work groups are task oriented, they are likely to move the coalition more effectively than other components of the coalition. According to Dluhy, the overall objective of the work group is to promote the coalition's active involvement in tasks that lead to optimal functioning. The various coalitions examined for this chapter used their respective work groups differently from coalition to coalition. In some instances, typically among those coalitions having smaller numbers, the executive board constituted the major work group. In other instances, appointed and elected officers and committee members constituted the primary work groups. Among the six work groups that Dluhy (1984) discusses, all were part of the efforts of the 10 coalitions studied. In addition, there were a number of other work groups (referred to in some of the 10 coalitions as "committees"). Table 7.6 represents Dluhy's listing in comparison with the coalitions studied.

Volunteer Work

An absolute positive aspect to any coalition is the degree of its volunteerism. Coalition members studied for this chapter reported an average of 6.5 hours per month expended on partnership business. Volunteer work involves the time and energies expended by a coalition member without compensation. Hence, persons working with a coalition who are on loan from their place of employment are not counted within this category (unless these individuals work beyond the hours that would normally be spent on their respective jobs). The work from volunteers in coalition building is not restricted to coalition members only. Often, volunteers are community residents who support the work of the coalition in an auxiliary capacity. This is particularly the case when special events or activities (e.g., health fairs) are carried out.

A SYSTEMS APPROACH

The development of coalitions in rural areas can promote an overall improved state of health for rural residents. Coalitions can enhance their respective

TABLE 7.6 Work Groups as Identified by Dluhy in Comparison With Project RECLAIM

Dluhy*	RECLAIM
Long-range planning and forecasting	Long-range planning
Talent and recruitment	Member recruitment
Communications	Communications
Special events	Special events
Monitoring and oversight	Internal monitoring
Media/public relations	External and public affairs

*Dluhy (1984).

geographical areas by extending the number of services provided and hence the number of persons reached; they also can promote a sense of solidarity and cohesion among residents. With residents collectively pursuing goals that benefit their neighborhoods (in this instance, the combating of drug abuse), a sense of community develops. If rural areas are to effectively develop their communities so that residents can enjoy a higher quality of life, they must be concerned with available health care services. Active coalitions in these areas facilitate an area's overall attractiveness, thereby increasing the chances of enticing physicians and other health care professionals who often elude these communities.

Although the populations in the coalitions studied stand in stark contrast to one model for promoting rural primary care practices, the Utah model (Sherwood, Porcher, & Hess, 1993) presents interesting findings that show the use of a *functional analysis systems technique* (FAST). This technique has been used in program planning and policy development to address certain problems. The Utah model, which includes a partnership between the Utah Department of Health and the University of Utah's Department of Family and Preventive Medicine and the College of Nursing, sought to provide access to primary health care for all rural Utah. In short, the Utah model appears to be successful for enhancing the life chances of rural residents in light of a real recognition of the importance of partnerships for effective planning. Acting on this recognition in the execution of a systems approach has helped to retain primary care providers in the respective rural areas.

The attraction and retention of primary care providers and other health care professionals are key indicators of a rural area's quality of life. The quality of life in rural areas is associated not only with the availability of professional health care but also with access to medical care. The shortage of physicians in rural areas continues to be a serious problem. Although incentives, including grants at the federal level, have added to the number of practicing physicians and other health care professionals in these areas, the demand for these care providers still exceeds the supply. Moreover, given setbacks to affirmative action, certain practices to attract physicians to rural areas are being threatened. For instance, the University of Georgia Medical School has extended the principle of affirmative action to include all rural applicants for medical school, regardless of race (U.S. Government Printing Office, 1992). This practice, however, could be struck down in the current wave of opposition to affirmative action.

Preventive, in addition to primary, health care is a dire need in black rural areas. In advancing health promotion and preventive medicine, coalitions and other partnerships have developed throughout various rural communities. Although the ultimate goal of the 10 coalitions studied in this chapter was substance abuse prevention, goals of other rural coalitions have ranged from cancer screening to HIV prevention. An important aspect to health planning in communities, both rural and urban, is input from the community on the type and nature of the activity to be undertaken. Funding agencies, sponsors, and program managers alike have recognized that efforts that have been sanctioned by community or coalition members tend to be more successful than those that are imposed on the community. These partners understand that the best way to determine what communities need is to ask those who live there. Listening to the community and planning strategies to enhance health based on community input are basic to successful coalition development. The Center for Substance Abuse Prevention's initiative, similar to those of other private organizations, recognizes that programs created by local citizens and tailored to meet local needs and resources are more likely to succeed and to continue operating than programs dictated by those outside the community. Given the importance of empowering the citizenry at the local level (Braithwaite, 1992), coalitions that are developed void of a community empowerment dimension often face cultural or other dilemmas that seriously impede the groups' work.

Health coalitions in rural areas emerge in response to the aforementioned shortage of health care personnel in addition to other concerns. In attempts to contain costs associated with quality health care and to address issues of access, coalitions seek to work with the existing health and medical services in a given community. Although many rural areas are dependent on state and national funds to subsidize health care costs, these areas are aware of the potential impact of private, community-level involvement. It is the coalition's task to present the issue of reform in a way that both business and government can buy into the benefits of such a plan and hence be willing to support the effort long-term. Subsequently, a given health or medical cause has an advantage of being more likely to endure, to be more well coordinated, and to have the desired impact and/or outcome.

The health care coalition movement, or the phenomenon that describes the advent and proliferation of coalitions across the country, is largely tied to deregulation—a shift from state and federal government cost containment efforts to local, private sector initiatives. According to McLaughlin et al. (1989), peak years of the health care coalition movement were 1982 and 1983. Although the needed empirical studies are too few to derive conclusive data on outcomes of coalitions and their prospects or to accurately project their magnitude, coalitions continue to be popular as vehicles for advancing health care causes. Especially in rural areas, coalitions are making their way into the lives of citizens and having an apparent impact. As evidenced from the voices of rural residents presented in this chapter as well as those documented in other case studies, the health care coalition movement is very much active.

Whether the problem in rural areas is one of bankrupt hospitals, insufficient number of health care practitioners, access to health care, or a related issue, coalitions have emerged to address these concerns. The benefits of coalition formation in rural areas are many. We have already seen how coalitions in a general way bolster the resources of a community. Regardless of the specific health-related goal, these alliances promote an individual cause more thoroughly than an organization can single-handedly. The systems approach, which considers the community's social, economic, professional, cultural, and other factors, fosters the meeting of the coalition's objectives. This model has been successfully implemented by a number of rural communities, both black and white (Sherwood et al., 1993). In addition, the theory-driven coalitions discussed in Chapter 3 (urban context) can be models for communities in search of partnerships that work. Goeppinger (1993) attests to the utility of theoretically derived partnerships between health care providers and rural residents. She surmises not only that theoretically based partnership interventions can be successful but also that they hold great potential to decrease individual health risks and create health-promoting environments in other communities. Whether derived via a theoretical or systems approach, or based on some other model, coalitions and their strategies offer much toward enhanced health for rural residents. Especially for black rural residents, the advent of coalitions signals a positive phenomenon in promoting health and wellness among this vulnerable population.

8

Sustaining and Maintaining Coalitions

As demonstrated, a coalition is typically a time-limited organization in which there is a convergence of interest from both individuals and organizations, centered on common goals. It is an organization of organizations that allows groups to become involved in new issues, without the necessity of managing or developing those emerging issues by themselves (Dluhy, 1990). As previously discussed, coalitions have historically functioned in the African American community, and mobilization around common interests has led to major victories. For example, during the civil rights movement, churches and other civic groups organized around a common interest and effected positive change.

Because a coalition is usually a temporary entity, the challenge lies in building one that can effectively address issues in a limited or stipulated period. The key is continual assessment of the costs and benefits of coalition participation by its members. Goals, resources, and relationships among people change continuously. Hence, it is important to evaluate the coalition regularly to ensure agreement by all parties (Dluhy, 1990). Coalitions must perceive themselves as self-supporting organizations that provide a needed service to the community, not as recipients of charitable contributions (Kennedy & Riley, 1986). Some coalitions are more capable than others of developing solutions, managing affairs, and providing support. Some coalitions and communities have a history of initiating action and organizing their membership to meet the needs of the community population. As depicted in the previous chapter, the Bartow County Coalition (in comparison with the other nine coalitions of Project RECLAIM) met its objectives largely through strong management and organizational skills.

DEVELOPING AND MAINTAINING COALITIONS

Much of the literature about coalitions is based on three assumptions: (1) The development of coalitions proceeds through definable stages; (2) the effectiveness of coalitions, measured by the implementation of programs and services and the accomplishment of long-term goals, is enhanced by organizational development of the coalition; and (3) coalition effectiveness is influenced by member satisfaction, participation, and commitment (McLeRoy, Kegler, Steckler, Burdine, & Wisotzky, 1994).

The driving force behind the formation of most coalitions is a timely and dramatic issue, which must be clearly articulated and developed. In the initial phases of development, most coalitions strive to gain credibility from the community, so that they will be perceived as a legitimate representative on an issue. Therefore, the first issue chosen by the coalition must have "marketing" appeal; it must be demonstrated to have relevance in the lives of residents. Coalition leaders must articulate an issue that galvanizes the community and invokes a community response (Dluhy, 1990).

There is relatively little consideration of the cultural, political, and organizational context within which newly formed coalitions develop and function, such as their history, the presence of other coalitions, the degree of cooperation and conflict among community agencies, and the potential effects of broad social and policy issues. It is too often believed that simply bringing people together to address common problems will have a positive impact on communities.

Coalition advocates discuss two means through which communities may benefit from the formation of a coalition: (1) implementation of structured activities to achieve a desired objective and (2) enhanced community capacity for problem solving. Implementation of structured activities depends on the extent to which coalition members and staff are capable of selecting, planning, and implementing interventions that will lead to specific outcomes and the extent to which these outcomes can be influenced by local actions. Enhancing community capacity is a community development approach. It depends on community participation and control and requires that residents define the problem and identify the types of intervention activities that are compatible with their culture and history. This may not always occur with externally funded coalitions, where the problem and acceptable approaches may be defined by agencies outside the community.

It is important to work with the existing social units—including families, social networks, organizations, neighborhoods—through which community members' day-to-day needs are met. If coalitions take over the role of existing organizations within communities, or substitute externally defined problems for community-defined ones, they may threaten, rather than increase, unity.

At the initial meeting of a new coalition, the overall goal and first task should be to establish an organizational framework that builds ownership and control while maintaining an open, flexible, direct-action focus. A second task at this first meeting is to establish the political purpose of the coalition. All members must agree on the political purpose of the coalition. The shared goal should not require members to give up their individual, professional or organizational/agency goals. The last task of the first meeting is to tentatively agree on the membership base of the coalition. In many coalitions, membership bases are mixed, with agencies, professionals, and community residents coming together (Dluhy, 1990). Coalitions must develop an organizational form; recruit, retain, and socialize new members; and develop and carry out a plan of action (McLeRoy et al., 1994). Serving simple refreshments, if possible, is a strategy for facilitating member attendance. This practice can and should develop as a social norm for the members, and they will begin to look forward to the available repast. The refreshments also provide an opportunity for members to engage in light social discussion on numerous issues.

An important indicator of coalition development and maintenance is the extent to which the coalition develops a separate organizational identity and organizational culture. This means that members shift from representing their own organizations in the coalition to working primarily for the coalition itself. This phenomenon is known as *cohesion*. Cohesive coalitions have a clear mission, goal statements, and well-defined administrative and decisionmaking procedures (McLeRoy et al., 1994).

Hierarchical structures in coalitions may pose significant barriers to broad community participation. Developers should also understand that unless a coalition is perceived by its members and the broader community as successful in addressing community problems, the coalition may lead to the disempowerment of communities. Coalition successes have the potential to demonstrate the effectiveness of working together to solve local problems. A failure, however, may similarly convince communities that partnerships are not effective and may increase skepticism about collaborative approaches (McLeRoy et al., 1994).

CHARACTERISTICS OF SUCCESSFUL COALITIONS

Coalition success is based partly on the member commitment of time and energy and the degree of formalization possessed by the group. Formalized rules and procedures, member organizational commitment, and staff satisfaction with the coalition are primary predictors of coalition success. Perceived effectiveness and activity levels also predict coalition success.

Successful coalitions recognize that a mix of incentives is necessary to sustain member interest. Coalitions that provide a wide array of incentives for participation will be more viable and go farthest in institutionalization and permanence. Broad-based coalitions that address a variety of concerns can rely on other activities and goals if their membership becomes burned out. Coalitions with a mix of goals are better able to adapt and sustain themselves through time (Dluhy, 1990).

McLaughlin et al. (1989) note several reasons why some coalitions are unsuccessful. Coalitions often disband because of apathy, conflict among members, and a lack of leadership as well as a shortage of success; the presence of a competing coalition; and the perception that costs outweigh the benefits. Coalitions should continuously assess when and under what circumstances involvement in a coalition will benefit the members.

A characteristic of successful coalitions is the ability to exploit various potential sources. Coalitions should also pay attention to the fundamental tasks of long-range planning, recruitment of members, and inter- and intra-coalition communication; design of special events; monitoring of legislative, bureaucratic, and fiscal changes affecting the coalition and its members; and media/ public relations (see Table 7.6). In successful coalitions, the leadership emphasizes both the task-oriented and interpersonal functions of the group (Dluhy, 1990). It assumes the responsibility of managing conflict within the coalition and maintaining its presence in the community.

It is essential to have members experience a sense of ownership of the coalition while at the same time keeping the process within the coalition open and flexible. The members should feel that they have an impact on the action plan and implementation (Johnson, 1993). Certain practices create harmonious internal operations and lead to successful coalitions: finding a place for everyone in the coalition, avoiding elitism in organizational structure, keeping issues in front of the members, having no hidden agendas, avoiding organizational rigidity, not becoming too formalized, rotating leadership positions or using a small but representative policy or steering committee, using periodic retreats and self-assessment techniques, not wasting members' time, stressing tasks with clear payoffs, stressing organizational and professional credibility above all else, downplaying individual personalities, designing political strategies that allow maximum participation among members, encouraging multiple rather than single strategies, and openly discussing covert political action in which members may be asked to participate but that they may find objectionable (Dluhy, 1990).

Successful coalitions manage conflict. As they refine and narrow their goals, disagreements among members are inevitable (McLeRoy et al., 1994). Coalition leaders should know how to manage conflict and facilitate collaboration among coalition factions so that members do not lose interest. Successful management of conflict also includes maintaining a sensitivity to the reasons coalition members participate in collaboration efforts. Leaders should remind members why they joined the coalition. Members may have joined the organization for ideological or symbolic beliefs; tangible benefits for the member's agency or profession; tangible benefits for the individual; social benefits for the individual; enhancement of agency or professional reputation; improvement of client situation; civic duty or pride; and critical up-to-date information and knowledge about clients, services, or the broader field (Dluhy, 1990). Reminding coalition members of their reasons for joining will minimize conflict as the coalition evolves and is essential to maintaining a successful coalition.

A community's history of interorganizational conflict or cooperation may also affect the development and functioning of coalitions. Communities characterized by intergroup and interorganizational conflict may have more difficulty in attracting members from segments of the community and developing coalition identity. For example, conflicts may manifest themselves in coalition meetings and discussions, resulting in difficulty in reaching consensus and performing tasks. Conversely, coalitions may provide a vehicle for addressing community conflicts and increasing interorganizational cooperation. Without sufficient information about the community context within which coalitions function, there are limited means to resolve preexisting community frictions (McLeRoy et al., 1994).

COALITION RENEWAL

Coalitions often lose sight of their *raison d'être,* jeopardizing the central mission of the coalition. Without an institutional embodiment of purpose, an organization may not be able to move on to its next stage of development. According to Dluhy (1990), when this happens, three strategies for renewal should be considered:

1. *A direct appeal to the membership about the problem or the clients being served:* Reassessment of purpose can reinvigorate the membership.

2. *Recruitment of new members:* Do the current members still have sufficient philosophical commitment to the coalition? Recruiting new members can stimulate enthusiasm and energy.

3. *Shifting efforts to another issue:* The move to a related issue can usually bring new members into the coalition. The coalition is a dynamic instrument for effecting change but may be unable to move to the next stage of development without an emphasis on renewal.

It is strongly recommended that coalitions develop a continuing socialization strategy for new as well as established members. Regular retreats, inservice training, workshops, and guest speakers educate coalition members as well as contribute to the sense of purpose of the collaboration. Members understand the mission of the coalition, how it operates in practice, and how strategies and tactics used by other groups can lead to success. Continuing education of the membership can reinforce dedication to the coalition. Dluhy (1990) captures one coalition leader's sentiments as follows:

> You cannot just keep asking people to help with the tasks of the coalition, you have to convince them that they are the coalition, and that they are in control of its destiny. They need to understand the issues, the people and the process. This is what education of the members means, and it pays off because the members stay and they eventually recruit others as well." (p. 59)

Continuing Recruitment

As stated previously, the recruitment of new members can stimulate new enthusiasm and energy. Continuing recruitment is essential to the life of community coalitions. When new coalition members are recruited, there is the expectation of social and behavioral interventions (i.e., coalitions) that people will participate in activities that will improve their own health and that of others. Goals for recruitment should include processes that are directed toward continuous development and strengthening of general coping abilities, competence, and self-confidence of those recruited (Stewart & Klitzner, 1993).

Emphasizing the tradition of self-help used by the African American community to effect change may enhance recruitment ability. Most African American self-help organizations historically used collective efforts aimed at social change, with an emphasis on individual competence and personal responsibility. The principles of self-help should be embraced by all segments of the African American community because they can be useful vehicles for developing adaptive responses to social problems. Those principles also apply when recruiting new membership into coalitions (Neighbors, Braithwaite, & Thompson, 1995).

Mentoring and Training of Coalition Members

Mentoring and training should focus on developing leadership skills for all members. Those who hold leadership positions must be technically and managerially competent. They must be effective communicators, motivators, and mobilizers of public opinion (Roper, Baker, Dyal, & Nicola, 1992).

Advocacy skills are the cornerstone of coalition building. Skills essential for active coalition members include persuasive personalities, knowing when to use pressure, strong commitment to coalition goals, ability to act for clients or advocate for a social problem, ability to compromise and negotiate, perseverance, patience, ability to listen, acting as a team player by being willing to go along with the majority of the coalition, and knowing when to push and when to back off.

Two methods can be employed to determine what type of skills training is needed. The first is a self-assessment by coalition members of their personal skills to determine their strengths and weaknesses. Members can be encouraged to attend workshops sponsored by coalitions or local universities to learn skills.

The second approach is to survey the tasks or activities in which members are willing to engage and how much time they are willing to commit to each. Tasks to be surveyed should include making telephone calls; writing letters or sending telegrams; preparing written documents; monitoring legislation, rules, and budget hearings; attending political strategy meetings; testifying before legislative committees; lobbying public officials directly; fundraising; working in an election campaign for a local elected representative; raising funds for a candidate in a state or local election; giving money directly to a state or local candidate; and soliciting fellow agency employees or board members to help lobby for the coalition (Dluhy, 1990). The leadership of the coalition must be careful in assigning coalition tasks so that certain members are not offended. Therefore, surveys of willingness to perform tasks should be analyzed so that the underlying philosophy of members is always apparent.

The CDC designed a strategy to support coalitions that provided intensive training to its members. Those programs include organizations such as the Association of Black Psychologists, which trained more than 40 psychologists to serve as AIDS education and support counselors; the National Medical Association, which provided regional training and established state AIDS task forces in member chapters to increase member involvement in prevention and intervention programs and their competence as HIV prevention authorities in black communities; the National Medical Association/Comprehensive Health Center, which developed train-the-trainer programs for HIV occupational risk prevention among black health professionals, law enforcement officers, fire-fighters, funeral directors, and morticians; Howard University, which developed a training program to improve HIV-related knowledge, awareness, and counsel-ing skills of black dentists and physicians followed by clinical nurses and physician's assistants; the Association for Drug Abuse Prevention and Treat-ment, Inc., which has developed training programs for agencies and organiza-tions nationwide on how to reach and intervene with people who inject drugs to control and prevent the spread of HIV infection; Logan Heights Family Health Center, which developed a manual to train staff members and selected clients to address HIV issues in a culturally relevant and sensitive way; the American Indian Health Care Association, which has developed culturally sensitive HIV and AIDS education and prevention materials for professional health care workers to use in working with urban American Indian populations; and the United Migrant Opportunity Services, which developed a program of technical assistance that includes training, outreach, and funding for HIV/AIDS projects of agencies serving migrants in the Midwest (Holman, Jenkins, Gayle, Carlton, & Lindsey, 1991). These coalitions have trained members in specific ways to address the needs of members of their communities.

FUNDRAISING

Some communities have difficulty meeting the basic needs of some segments of their population. Sufficient resources may not be available locally to fund new initiatives, or even to support existing programs. Even when coalitions receive support from external sources, there still may not be enough to address community needs. Moreover, some coalition members may participate in coalitions simply to secure additional resources for their own organization, undermining the goal of maximizing commitment to the coalition (McLeRoy et al., 1994).

Although it is common to look to government for financial support for many human services, increasingly foundations, the voluntary sector, the private sector, and individual donors are also being turned to for support. Although it may be advantageous for an individual organization to seek its own funding, there are many circumstances in which joint action or a partnership among organizations may be more desirable. Nongovernment sources have frequently encouraged proposals submitted by groups of organizations in the community. Many projects can be funded in communities in which organizations are linked through partnerships. There are also circumstances in which an application for funding is substantially enhanced by having a group of organizations as the applicant. Organizations that are able to collaborate successfully in nonpolitical arenas, as in seeking nongovernment resources, will find it easier to collaborate in political arenas.

Members of an organization should ask themselves a number of questions when they are contemplating a joint application:

- Has the funding source designated that joint applications are either preferred or required?

- Will the organization receive a clear set of tangible benefits if this application is funded?

- Will joint efforts ease the development of the proposal application because of shared resources and expertise?

- Will the joint application enhance the probability of being funded?

- Will benefits of the partnership reach into other areas in the future?

Projects that are specifically aimed at improving cooperation and coordination in the community between organizations and service providers are examples of the types of projects for which joint funding applications for new programs are possible (Dluhy, 1990).

In 1987, the CDC awarded funds to state and local health departments specifically for health education and risk reduction in racial and ethnic minority populations. The grants were the first funds provided by CDC directly to racial and ethnic minority national consortia. This effort was complemented in 1989 by direct funding of community-based organizations, with 50% of the funds ($5 million) designated for minority community-based organizations. Funding these local consortia was part of an effort to involve greater numbers of minority community leaders, professionals, institutions, and agencies in HIV and AIDS information dissemination and to stimulate programs that tap into a variety of national, regional, and community resources in a coordinated way. It was also expected that at the end of the funding period, institutional structures for preventing HIV infection among racial and ethnic minorities would be stronger.

Making funds available for a specific purpose is often used as a mechanism by funding sources for encouraging the development of coalitions. For example, to increase the number of organizations in HIV prevention, the CDC-sponsored grants encouraged the formation of new national and regional consortia of minority service organizations. Organizations that could address the education needs of racial and ethnic minority populations in the United States and its territories were encouraged to apply (Holman et al., 1991).

Fundraising is an essential, although undeveloped, activity. Changing economic and sociological patterns have forced institutions to reassess their structures and to search for new sources of financial support, and coalitions are no different. There is no shortcut for developing and implementing an effective fundraising strategy. Fundraising is a developmental process that begins with organizational assessment. Why should financial support be provided to this organization? An element of developing the foundation for successful fundraising efforts is a statement of the case for support. In addition to the potential benefits of the coalition in general, specific reasons should be identified why individuals, foundations, corporations, and governments should select the coalition for financial support. If other coalitions provide similar services in the community, the coalition needs to clarify how it stands out. Because fundraising is continual, a blueprint for the future of the organization is integral to setting goals that reflect both immediate and future needs. Common sources of gifts are individuals, corporations, foundations, clubs and other organizations, civic groups, and the government (Jones, 1991).

Many people provide financial support to coalitions because of a perceived moral obligation, the personal satisfaction of helping others, or guilt. Generally, giving reflects cultural patterns, values, and traditions and can also play a crucial role in self-identification and the development of a sense of belonging to a desired community. Participation in fundraising is also one of the socially sanctioned ways of facilitating upward mobility. In many businesses, fundraising activity not only is expected but also is used to evaluate promotability.

Developing financial resources requires pursuing funds from multiple sources using a variety of techniques. Fundraising requires a systematic approach geared toward the maintenance and growth of the coalition. The leader of the coalition must create a setting for confidence building that will influence persons both inside and outside the collaboration to share in the coalition's sense of commitment and mission (Jones, 1991).

A coalition must spend money to raise money. Because nothing is more crucial to the future of a coalition than the ability to generate financial support, fundraising activities should receive priority on the coalition budget. In any fundraising effort, it is important to acknowledge the source of the contribution. If formal recognition of giving behavior provides motivation to continue giving, then any gift requires acknowledgment. This can be done by listing donors by categories in the annual report, displaying donors' names prominently in the building, or awarding plaques with donors' names and relationships to the coalition.

Corporate Fundraising

Corporate fundraising, as one aspect of fundraising in the private sector, deserves special consideration. Corporate giving is a little-used resource because it is a difficult area for the newcomer to tap and because donations are based partly on past contributions, industry comparisons, and profits. Corporate philanthropy operates on the principle that "corporate fruit does not fall far from the corporate tree." Corporate donations are usually given in the geographic area in which the company or its affiliates are located or to organizations that purchase the corporation's services. Corporations generally give a higher percentage to health and welfare than do private donors. Cash grants by corporations tend to be small, and recipients are usually well-established, secure, and noncontroversial. Contributions other than cash should be considered; any product the corporation sells or makes can benefit the coalition. Using other aspects of the corporation's operations is another option; services such as printing and advertising can yield large savings. Corporations may also lend executives to provide technical assistance, and volunteers may influence other corporate personnel to look favorably on the coalition as well.

In conclusion, fundraising is crucial to the life of the coalition. Fundraising skills should be developed and resources exploited. The key to success is to mobilize what is known about human behavior and motivation into effective fundraising activity (Jones, 1991).

RECOGNITION OF CONSTITUENCY ACCOMPLISHMENTS

It is important to recognize the accomplishments of coalition constituency. The attainment of goals gives coalition members a sense of achievement and creates energy to face other challenges. One of the critical tasks of leadership is to ensure sufficient incentives to sustain coalition participation. Recognition of accomplishments and gains achieved by the coalition helps strengthen coalition cohesion and sustainability.

Accomplishments may be acknowledged in a variety of ways. Some organizations use plaques with constituents' names. Others recognize constituents in the media. Still others use activities such as dinners and luncheons to retain interest and convey to constituents that their work is appreciated. Regardless of the method, recognition of accomplishments keeps constituents' spirits high and solidifies their commitment to the organization.

STRATEGIES IN ESTABLISHING STABLE COALITION PARTNERSHIPS

According to Butterfoss et al. (1993), the degree of formalization of coalitions is related to successful collaboration. Rogers et al. (1993) found that formalized rules and procedures predicted two intermediary measures of coalition/partnership success: member organization commitment and staff satisfaction with the coalition. Stable partnerships are correlated with perceived effectiveness and perceived activity levels of the group, and strong leadership is correlated with coalition stability. Strong central leadership, communication and interpersonal skills, competence in negotiation and problem solving, and administrative ability are characteristics of a leader who can maintain coalition partnerships for the long term. Other leadership characteristics include an empowering leadership style that is related to coalition effectiveness, including member satisfaction, member knowledge, quality of coalition work plans, and perceptions of coalition effectiveness (McLeRoy et al., 1994).

According to Johnson (1993), some experts predict that the rate of coalition development will subside. Instead, coalitions in multiple-coalition areas will begin to join together to further increase their power within the community. Other predictions for the future of partnerships include these: (a) Partnerships, as they become more stable, will become more professional with larger operating budgets and a paid staff; (b) partnerships will expand their influence beyond the local community; (c) partnerships will increase their involvement in health planning activities; (d) many partnerships will become public policy forums in which key players merge to formulate policy directions; and (e) other partnerships may evolve into professional associations with professional development and education as their primary goal.

Stability of coalition partnerships depends largely on the stability of the environment in which the coalition exists. A highly unstable environment means that organizations will often find coalitions useful, because they allow the organizations to join groups and find partners for collaborative purposes. Alternately, stable and predictable environments can be characterized by the already established patterns of interaction. There is little incentive under these circumstances to join a coalition unless the current patterns of collaboration are judged as undesirable or there is a profound political issue. There are, in short, few incentives to join a coalition in a stable environment.

Because coalitions are typically temporary entities, little has been written about the problems of building and maintaining them. In trying to determine what leads to stable partnerships, however, we can examine factors that lead to coalition dissolution. An integral part of the definition of coalitions is that they must act as a group, either through a group action or through concerted member action (i.e., dividing tasks and allocating them to individual members). Group action is a fundamental characteristic of coalitions that distinguishes them from purely social or reference groups that might commiserate about common problems. If members never take joint or orchestrated action, they cannot be considered a coalition.

Stable coalition partnerships are issue oriented, develop an external focus, are deliberately constructed, and take concerted action. Because coalitions rely more on emergent social interaction rather than on formally prescribed rules to define membership, the boundaries may be ill defined. Because of the lack of formal rules and structure, the existence of the coalition is likely to be temporary. Stable partnerships, therefore, have formal rules and structure.

Stable partnerships are more likely to occur when the coalition obtains a larger resource allocation than the individual partners could on their own. If the benefits of staying together are greater than operating independently, the likelihood of a stable partnership is great. Stable partnerships have greater opportunities for member interaction. Coalitions are more likely to become stable if members have been a part of a coalition before. Individuals with previous experience in a coalition are more likely to form new coalitions than individuals with no experience (Stevenson et al., 1985).

The study of coalition termination also helps us understand what it means to institutionalize coalition-based efforts in communities. If institutionalization— as opposed to maintenance—is the extent to which a program is embedded and becomes an integral part of the host community, it is logical to assume that coalitions become institutionalized in any of several ways. First, they may be successful in securing external, stable sources of funding either through an incorporated status or from nonprofit organizations with broad community support. Second, existing agencies may provide previously coalition-sponsored services as the coalition itself terminates. Third, a coalition may be adopted by a host agency and become integrated into its structure (McLeRoy et al., 1994).

THE ESTABLISHMENT OF REPRESENTATION

Many coalitions, especially those receiving funding from outside sources, emphasize the importance of representation from multiple community sources. If a coalition consisting primarily of representatives from various community organizations is successful in developing a formal and effective organizational structure, however, community residents may inadvertently be prevented from participating in the coalition. To effectively participate in an organization, individuals must have an understanding of its culture, structure, and procedures. Community representatives without experience in working in formal bureaucracies may find it difficult to learn within the constraints imposed by the organization. Moreover, community residents may be intimidated by professionals in the coalition (McLeRoy et al., 1994). Community residents should be prepared for full participation in coalitions; otherwise, they may decide to discontinue their involvement.

One of the purported advantages of coalitions is that they provide a means for recruiting individuals from diverse constituencies, such as political, business, human services, and social and religious groups, as well as grassroots groups and individuals. Some concern has been expressed, however, about the true representation of groups in coalitions. Florin, Mitchell, and Stevenson (1995) reported that members of a Rhode Island coalition were predominantly white, and the large proportion of members were from human service agencies and schools. Similarly, Rogers et al. (1993) identified a number of groups, including ethnic minorities, medical and dental professionals, businesses and workshops, and youth, that were poorly represented in the California tobacco control coalitions. In another study, Herman, Wolfson, and Forster (1993) found that membership in a family planning coalition was based on existing networks, with the majority of members having worked together in the past. Although building coalitions based on existing networks can lead to rapid mobilization, it may leave significant gaps in membership. Through time, coalitions may expand to include a broader constituency (McLeRoy et al., 1994). This representation is essential to building and sustaining coalitions in the African American community.

9

Building Community-Developed Coalitions
A Practical Approach

Many models exist for coalition building, and many African American communities across the United States have decided to support and engage in community-based partnerships as a foundation for their collaborative efforts. Other organizations have worked to glean narratives and stories from across the country describing various process steps in organizing communities to engage in tasks designed to improve the quality of life of local residents.

Recently, some organizations, such as the HealthCare Forum, have formed a compendium of *Best Practices in Creating Healthier Communities and Populations* (Johnson et al., 1996). Other community-developed partnerships, both public and private, have been based on community organization and development literature, whereby models with their subsequent process steps have been identified. These models include, but are not limited to, approaches developed by Florin (Florin, Mitchell, & Stevenson, 1995); Lofquist (1989); Braithwaite (1992); Putnam (1994); Kretzman & McKnight (1993); Fawcett (1993); the Assessment Protocol for Excellence in Public Health (APEX-PH, 1991); CDC's (1993d) Planned Approach to Community Health (PATCH); and the seven core processes of emerging best practices (Cohen, Baer, & Satterwhite, 1991; Himmelman, 1994).

From these models and constructs, some general themes can be drawn. First, community organization and development are more art than an exact science that adheres to pure experimental design. Second, coalitions are alliances among different community sectors, organizations, and grassroots groups for a common purpose, and they often reflect the norms and values of self-help, local control, and citizen action of the community in which they are initiated. Third, the "community" should be the impetus for the effort of coming together to organize and do something new. This is where real community empowerment, as opposed to betterment, takes place (Himmelman, 1994). In this how-to section of the book, empowerment is emphasized as a process whereby individuals gain control over their destiny. Fourth, the importance of starting with a common frame of reference (e.g., deciding on what collaborating is or is not) will require listening to the voices of the community. Himmelman describes collaboration as exchanging information, altering activities, sharing resources, and enhancing the capacity of another for mutual benefit and to achieve a common purpose. Developing this level of synergy in a community is one challenge. Achieving results as a direct causal chain from community action that leads to community change is the other hurdle. Fifth, community organization and development take time and resources, a point that is emphasized throughout this book. Time commitments by coalition members, however, have been shown to be a sustaining force for coalition maintenance and survival.

Organizing communities to do anything is rarely a quick fix, and tools for developing timelines will be helpful. Steps or processes within these various models or frameworks have been compared for similarities and differences. As a result, commonalities or themes have begun to emerge with respect to process steps:

Step 1: Identify issue/concern/topic (assets mapping or developing indicators could occur here).

Step 2: Identify gatekeepers/stakeholders/agencies (formal and informal community leaders).

Step 3: Develop mission/purpose/shared vision (e.g., articles of incorporation, memorandum of understanding).

Step 4: Develop guiding principles including decision-making and action teams or committees.

Step 5: Analyze and gain consensus about the work to be done.

Step 6: Map assets/build relationships (other models place this step at the beginning).

Step 7: Communicate/share information (includes member training activities).

Step 8: Do the work.

Step 9: Perform continuous quality improvement/process evaluation as well as impact and outcome evaluation where appropriate.

With these steps in mind, this how-to section is not a recipe in which precise inputs will guarantee expected results. Nor does it represent a baseline of performance data. This chapter does, however, point to how local public health practitioners working predominantly with African American communities in more than 30 counties in Georgia have implemented community-developed initiatives for health and prevention using a community organization and development approach (Braithwaite, Murphy, Lythcott, & Blumenthal, 1989). In large part, understanding the structure of these community-developed efforts was paramount to laying the foundation for population-based community health promotion and prevention.

Although coalition building has become a popular approach, the concept of coalition building is not new, as has been previously discussed. The approaches to coalition building, however, have assumed recent controversy.

For example, important differences exist between a community-developed approach and a community-based approach. The former emphasizes enhancement of economic development infrastructures and typically results in more long-lasting changes in the community (such as building a community center). The latter approach focuses on a community's strengths and looks to the community itself for solutions. The difference can also be seen in the processes of mapping of community assets (inventorying resources) as opposed to needs assessment work. According to Kretzman and McKnight (1993), the call to the traditional path of community assessment is a needs-driven, deficit-oriented approach that draws images of needy and deficient neighborhoods. As a result, this approach advocates that these neighborhoods can be rescued only by professionals and agencies. This approach has not been embraced by progressive and culturally grounded African American social scientists.

Each community has learned common knowledge resources that are available, as well as those that are less obvious. These are resources that come primarily in two packages: capacities and competencies. In other words, what can communities do, and how can they do it? Do communities come together just to fix problems? Many times, they come together to excel. So the *how* can be categorized in two ways: as community-based or community-developed. Thus, in a community-based approach, communities work to focus on problem solving by addressing perceived challenges.

The primary vehicle for change in a community-developed approach, on the other hand, is to build community control and ownership for improving social conditions. This approach has more long-term benefit and integrity for addressing quality-of-life issues in African American communities. This includes increasing resources and capacity for political and economic change as opposed to common information sharing, mass education, providing services, and working directly with individuals (not community groups). The primary decision makers in the community-developed approach are indigenous, informal, and elected leaders, not agency experts and other officials. These individuals typically function as community organizers. Community organizers play an important role as gadflies for stimulating community change initiatives. These changes are buttressed by understanding the ecology of community behavior.

ECOLOGY OF COMMUNITY BEHAVIOR

In most low-income communities nationwide (and many African American communities are low income), there exist a certain rhythm and distinguishing markers. Although unique in and of themselves, certain types of storefronts and curb stores tend to be found in certain places in every low-income community that are not commonly found in more established areas. In addition, there is a tendency toward patterns of high-risk streets where drugs are bought and sold and certain corners where the "brothers" regularly convene. Public transportation systems are also used extensively. These are some of the factors characterizing the ecology of many low-income urban communities—factors that determine "who wins" and "who loses" in the community on a day-to-day basis, as well as health risks and whether health interventions succeed or fail in the long haul. Program planners must take into account these realities when developing the community organization and development framework.

EMPHASIS ON EVALUATION OF
COALITION ACTIVITIES

Through the collection of coalition-building models from across the country, hybrid or integrated models have been implemented for work in diverse communities. Some of these models have taken on a community-based character; others, a community-developed quality. In addition to processing this material, those working in community organization and development should develop evaluation components to measure process, impact, and outcomes. In this particular example, *impact* not only means knowledge, skills, attitudes, beliefs, and abilities of participants in the effort but also can include the community's understanding of the coalition's function (as well as how the coalition sees itself). *Outcomes* include what the coalition set out to accomplish as well as the sustainability and maturity of the coalition and its action(s) in the community. These types of activities have resulted in new local community collaboratives that are currently in various stages of development. These experiences show that progress from one process to the next is often not linear or even cyclical. Progress often takes a circuitous route and flows through process steps based on an infinite number of variables in the human equation found in the context of community.

UNCERTAIN DEFINITION OF COMMUNITY

The definitions of *community* can be numerous, to include geography, ethnicity, and political and sexual persuasion, among others. Definitions of community can be broad (where a community group is coordinating an effort), and, at the same time, these associations of people must at some level organize their efforts. Confusion can result from uncertain and nebulous definition of community. Representation of the community interest is typically challenged by those not involved or by those whose roles may be threatened or challenged. Structure is imperative in any community work, especially when a community wishes to go beyond the level of networking or simple information sharing, in which adjusting calendars so people can attend the same meetings is the process for reaching the goal of capturing information. Furthermore, if the goal is to develop a cohesive collaboration that works to achieve community change, then the community may choose to engage various cross-sector participants to work for the same purpose so that everyone may succeed. With true collaboratives, if the one participant succeeds, all succeed—if the coalition succeeds, the community succeeds as well.

ISSUE OWNERSHIP

A community-developed framework to building a collaborative means approaching a community empty-handed, rather than harboring a hidden agenda or having a grant in hand. It means trust personified in groups. Furthermore, to approach an African American community with a defined plan in hand is to increase the perception that planning has already taken place and that including the community has become a secondary organizational need. Unfortunately, such has been the experience in many African American communities. Of course, the impetus or initiation must begin somewhere. The best conditions for developing successful community coalitions occur when the community is the spark or catalyst for starting the process. Hence the community owns the issue(s).

When the community brings its concerns and issues to agencies first, genuine empowerment and long-lasting initiatives stand a much greater chance of success and long-term sustainability. Community empowerment has been defined as "a process whereby groups increase their control over consequences that are important to their members and to others in the broader community" (Fawcett, Seekins, Whang, Muiu, & Suarez de Balcazar, 1984, p. 146).

As discussed in preceding chapters, many collaboratives have existed for some time, whereas others are just forming. Some of these include strategic alliances and partnerships of two or three stakeholders from various sectors of the community (e.g., faith, public, and private) as well as coalitions with many metrowide stakeholders and other communitywide efforts. African American communities must decide what steps they will take to organize themselves, thus embracing a self-determination philosophy. During the past 15 to 20 years, African American collaborating communities/groups have formalized their initiatives into legal entities. Most have incorporated as for-profit or not-for-profit organizations. For the latter, acquiring tax-exempt status (IRS 501[c]3) is seen as a necessary process linked to the fundraising and grant solicitation process. This essential step helps build the coalition infrastructure and jump-start its empowerment goals. The use of consultants from academic institutions and corporations who provide technical assistance and serve as collaborating partners is useful to the coalition when filing for technical designations such as federal tax-exempt status.

The National Coalition for Healthy Cities and Healthy Communities in the United States evolved from the World Health Organization. Currently, approximately 1,300 communities are participating in this Healthy Communities movement.[1] Leonard Duhl, M.D., one of the initiators of the Healthy Cities program, encourages persons engaged in this work to do the following:

> Define the program. All I say is that you have to start someplace. You have to begin to look at it in an ecological and systematic way. You have to involve people. You have to start thinking of values of equity and participation. Beyond that you can start wherever you want. (personal correspondence, April 1988)

Informal community networks and associations wishing to begin the process to become a collaborative and achieve long-term community change will need to focus on causes, rather than symptoms. Put another way, collaborative efforts, as a general principle, ought to focus on the determinants of health, rather than the symptoms of health problems per se. Determinants of health are those things that allow for conditions so that communities can be either healthy or unhealthy. But they can also be elements influencing individual health status, including lifestyle, services, environment, heredity, physiology, and political socioeconomic factors.

In this sense, the focus for change is on the conditions that allow for the initiation of risky health behaviors. In contrast is an example of one community that implemented a plan to eliminate graffiti. Community members did not consider the determinants of health as something to be addressed. Hundreds of persons were mobilized one weekend to paint over all the "tags" written on walls, overpasses, roads, buses, and so on. After the work had been done, a community celebration was attended by all those who had participated. Two weeks later, all the graffiti returned with a vengeance. Several reasons for this short-lived success may be obvious. Instead of developing prevention programs, inviting the youth involved in writing the graffiti to problem solve, or addressing the conditions that allow teens to achieve their self-esteem by participating in such behavior, the community focused on the symptoms.

Critical to the success of a collaborative will be who participates and why persons are participating. The following nine process steps will help communities to benefit from the lessons already learned about coalition-building processes.

STEP 1: IDENTIFY ISSUE/CONCERN/TOPIC

In "Developing Effective Coalitions: An Eight-Step Guide," Cohen et al. (1991) begin with the notion that "a coalition is not appropriate in every situation and is only one of a variety of tools for accomplishing organizational goals" (p. 5). Most of us are well aware of the problems facing our communities. We can scarcely pick up a newspaper without reading a seemingly infinite list of perceived and actual problems: increasing violence, hate crimes, crumbling infrastructure, racism, inadequate and unaffordable housing, low voter turnout, high teenage pregnancy rates, infant prematurity and mortality, and so on.

What strategy for change works best in addressing these issues? The health of the community is influenced, and indeed determined, by the conditions that contribute to health. Promotion of wellness and prevention of disease and injury are powerful community tools for improving health status. Therefore, it will be an important first step to assess the situation before moving forward. Not only does assessment provide an initial reference point, but also it helps in the development of a shared vision and subsequent steps. This should happen on two fronts: determining (1) what already exists and what is currently being done in a community and (2) what data and information are being drawn on to prioritize actions to be done. The next question of who is involved will come in the second step.

Many communities engage in community organization and development and collect primary or secondary data before taking actions that have impact on the determinants of their health. This might include reportable epidemiological data. Other important trends for developing a picture might include time trends and geographic distribution of health problems. When trends are moving in favorable directions, communities should seek out the factors that contribute to these outcomes and attempt to increase such efforts. Geographic analysis brings the opportunities for prevention closer to home. Recognition of the major health concerns in neighborhoods is the necessary first step toward positive action. Organized efforts undertaken by groups that truly know assets, strengths, and needs of their community will improve health status. After all, knowledge is power. An informed community has more power to act effectively for its own improvement. In many communities, a thorough assessment can present overwhelming needs and can fragment an emerging coalition. Thus, it will be critical to prioritize the needs for action.

Data Collection and Translation

In disenfranchised African American communities, consistent reinforcement concerning "ownership" is required when gathering information and data. Suspicion runs high in the black community when someone begins to gather information and ask questions. Therefore, community leaders should be constantly rallied to inform them of the importance of each phase of the data collection process and how this is *their* data to help them in building programs to improve quality of life and to solve problems in the community. Community leaders should be trained how to gather certain types of data and how to assist researchers and program specialists in the collection of significant data. This is key to the translation process. All data analysis must be conducted with a protocol for translation of the information into a form that community persons can fully understand. These data should be compiled and presented in a fashion digestible even to persons with little education. Descriptive statistics (pie and line charts and bar graphs) have been successfully used in many community coalition efforts to accomplish this goal.

Methods of analyses might include birth and death data from official birth and death certificates, usually obtained from state centers for health statistics or state and county health departments; population estimates based on U.S. Census of the Population data (although these are done at the end of each decade); and infant mortality rates computed per 1,000 live births, all birthrates per 1,000 population, or mortality rates per 100,000 population. Excess deaths or the years of potential life lost and other rates can be used to show comparative causes of premature death for specific populations. These can be calculated per 100,000 population between the ages of 1 and 64. This information, averages for infant mortality and cause-specific premature mortality, can be depicted on a geographic map of a defined area by census tract. The causes selected for depiction might include those conditions that were relatively high in rank for any of the race or gender groups. For example, maps might depict data for HIV/AIDS, unintentional injuries, cancer, homicide, heart disease, suicide, and stroke.

It is critical, however, to measure more than just problems. Traditionally, problem measurement has been the result of a community needs assessment. Many times, this type of information focuses primarily on quantitative objective data. A new coalition, however, may want to use assets mapping instead.

Assets mapping refers to an inquiry into the individual's, the institution's, and the community's capacity for prevention. In other words, what resources are available that either are or could be used for prevention? For example, schools and faith institutions could provide meeting space, and educators could provide facilitation skills. The purpose, as John Kretzman and John McKnight (1993) have written in their book *Building Communities From the Inside Out: A Path Toward Finding and Mobilizing a Community's Assets,* is to connect people with capacities. This provides emerging coalitions with a great advantage. Assets mapping might also include data collected via interviews, public opinion surveys, and community focus groups. Such an approach has particular relevance for coalition building in African American communities and builds on the strengths, rather than the weaknesses, that exist in communities.

Whatever the collaborative decides to assess, it should be information that can be measured through time. If information is trackable, it can indicate a trend. This step is as critical as everything to follow (i.e., vision, mission, goals, objectives, action steps, implementation, monitoring, evaluation, etc.) and will point back to what the collaborative decided to measure or attempted to change.

STEP 2: IDENTIFY GATEKEEPERS/ STAKEHOLDERS/AGENCIES

Before initiating a coalition, it is important to determine what already exists and is being done in a community. This includes knowing who is doing the work, who makes things happen, and who are the gatekeepers in a particular community. Have they already formed related groups involved with implementing preventive activities in the community? What informal or formal networks already exist? Are people already involved in strategies for change such as citizen participation, mass mobilization, education, social action, and other typologies (more of this in Step 8)? What roles do people already play in the community? Who are the leaders as identified by the people per se? This step draws attention to "taking stock" vis-à-vis a community resource inventory.

Once a seedbed for a coalition has been identified (e.g., local community groups, neighborhoods, parent-teacher associations, faith groups, and agencies), then the work of defining the type of coalition, or the need for a coalition, can begin. Will this coalition be a formal or informal collection of persons? Will this need to be time limited and ad hoc, single issue-oriented, agency-based, grassroots-led, community-based, or professionally based? An agency-based group is made up predominantly of agency representatives. It can be diverse with persons from various disciplines forming the group. In general, its purpose is to improve service delivery through collaborative efforts.

A grassroots coalition can be informal indeed. Usually, this is a group or groups made up of parents, neighbors, or others who share a nonprofessional concern for the community. Its primary aim is to organize and mobilize the group itself so that shared concerns in the community can be addressed. An example of this action is a neighborhood watch group.

A community-based coalition consists of a combination of representatives from community organizations, neighbors, and parents and can include local service agency representation. A professionally based coalition is composed of people who work in the same or similar professions. The primary purpose of the group is professional development.

Who will be invited to come to the table? Who will do the inviting? Why would they be interested in coming? What will be the extent of their involvement? Once the initial phone calls, letters, and recruitment have taken place, a plan for the initial participation activity should be defined. One tool for participation that has proved successful has been conducting a community "windshield survey." Here, teams drive throughout a particular route or community, and participants describe and record what their five senses tell them about the area, with respect to both strengths and challenges or weaknesses. Foci include elements such as infrastructure, housing, transportation, and clean air and water. Each vehicle follows a specified course, with team members identifying various housing patterns, businesses, schools, recreation facilities, and so forth. Within each group, one person records the discussion. Following meetings build on these discussions, with groups sharing observations about their community. To harness the momentum from these meetings, the group decides to establish a purpose and to ensure that they have stakeholders from throughout the community. The group could then facilitate the implementation of Paul Florin's community wheel exercise (see Figure 9.1).[2]

There are potential participants for each of the previously identified sectors (see Figure 9.2). Next, the group examines the depth of participation. In other words, did an individual attending a meeting represent him- or herself or an organization? For example, if local schools were identified as an important sector to include in the collaborative, did the invited attendee represent the superintendent's office? Was it the superintendent him- or herself? Did the individual speak for the school board? Could the individual make decisions and commit resources on behalf of an entire school district or an individual classroom, as in the case of a teacher perhaps? Or does the person simply represent him- or herself as a concerned citizen, and the person should not be included in the school sector at all? The group uses the wheel as a visual tool to identify different sectors and organization participation critical to the success of the coalition's formulation. The next step is to see if these tools will be helpful in making certain that participants are from all the sectors of the community. At this point, this is the most important task to accomplish. The success of the effort will hinge on engaging the right mix of people. Although power brokers and decision makers who are influential citizens ought to be included, they are

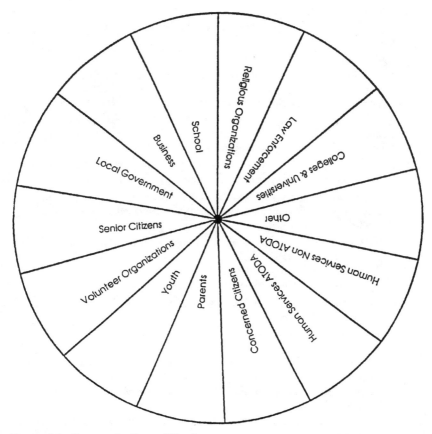

Figure 9.1. Community Sector Wheel

SOURCE: From *A Developmental Approach to Identifying Training and Technical Assistance Needs in Community Coalitions* (p. 5), by P. Florin, R. Mitchell, and J. Stevenson, May 1995. Paper presented at the National Conference on Health Promotion and Health Education, Atlanta, Georgia. Reprinted with permission.

not to make decisions for the entire community. Diversity is critical to collaboration, and pseudorepresentation will inevitably backfire and lead to sabotage.

STEP 3: DEVELOP MISSION/PURPOSE/ SHARED VISION

In this third step, participants develop together a picture of what their healthy community should look like. Through the use of facilitation tools and techniques, this picture should culminate into a shared vision or a goal. This

Instructions

Leader:

1. Explain:

    This wheel represents your community. It is divided into all the different sectors that make up our community.

    Are there any sectors that are not appropriate for our community? Have we left any out?

2. Explain:

    We want to see how well our coalition represents our whole community.

3. Give each member of your coalition a brown figure. Ask each to physically go to the wheel and place the figure in the sector that he or she represents.

4. When they are finished, ask members to think about whether they are there as individuals or if they represent an organization. The way to determine that is to ask themselves some questions:

    Q: When you vote, do you vote the way you personally would, or the way your organization would?

    Q: Do you speak for your organization?

    Q: Can you make decisions for your organization?

    If people do not know which sector they represent, they should put themselves in the Concerned Citizen sector.

5. Then ask your coalition members each of the following questions, allowing plenty of time to discuss them.

    a. What observations do you have about how broadly your current membership represents your whole community?

    b. What observations do you have about sectors for which there is no representative?

    c. What observations do you have about sectors with more than one representative?

    d. What observations do you have about the role of those representatives?

    e. What does an organization bring to the table that an individual cannot?

Setting Goals to Improve Mobilization:

1. Place a green (for growth) figure in any sector from which you want to seek representation.

2. Place a green triangle behind any of those you want to represent an organization or a whole sector.

3. If any current members want to go from sitting on the coalition as an individual to representing an organization or sector, place green triangles behind their figures.

Figure 9.2. Tool for Task #1: Mobilization

SOURCE: Adapted from *A Developmental Approach to Identifying Training and Technical Assistance Needs in Community Coalitions* (p. 4), by P. Florin, R. Mitchell, and J. Stevenson, May 1995. Paper presented at the National Conference on Health Promotion and Health Education, Atlanta, Georgia.

statement should compel people to action, but it should also be anchored into tangible indicators such as trends and geography (see Step 1). The goal should be supported by objectives that are carried out via action plans. This action(s) should lead to something new that has been previously supported by goals that all participants have had a stake in not only developing but implementing as well. The actual development of action planning will take place in the fourth step. How to influence a diverse group of people to grasp the same vision for the future, as well as how to get there, is a core competency for those engaged in facilitation. Although as a general rule, facilitators ought to be neutral in input, their role usually consists of keeping the group focused, on time, and on task. Therefore, they are catalysts of the process.

A facilitator working to build a collaborative should be a resource for the group, rather than an expert. A master facilitator, according to Fran Rees (1991), "views teamwork as an ongoing negotiation among diverse individuals who are all working toward common goals." Facilitators must be vigilant in keeping meetings on task. According to Rees, the four obstacle categories are these: "no clear meeting objectives or purpose; ineffective meeting processes; no closure or follow-up; and disorganization in planning or running the meeting" (p. 73).

One commonly used facilitation technique is a brainstorming modification whereby members of the group are asked to write down their definition of a healthy African American community. All written statements are displayed for everyone to see. The facilitator reads each one aloud without judgment or discussion. Then the statements are grouped by likeness. These likeness group- ings will define categories with various degrees of separation. At this point, although a decision-making mode has not been defined by the group, the facilitator ought to strive for consensus around a vision statement that is made cohesive by linking the previously defined categories. It may also be helpful to develop a subcommittee or action team to take the work at this point, further refine it, and bring it back for any amendments and final acceptance. Whatever mission, vision, or goal statement is developed, the group should be careful to set itself up not as a threat to member organizations or participants but as an enhancement of the work already being done (if others are doing similar work). Of course, this assumption is based on whether the particular community in question has the capacity to do the work.

Objectives should support the vision statement. An objective is a specific, measurable outcome of the action or program. An objective should offer some solutions to issues and challenges. Each objective should describe problem- related outcomes of the program. It should not describe methods but should define the following: the population served, the time when the objective will be met, and the objective or improvement in numerical terms. Objectives that are measurable become the criteria by which to judge the effectiveness of the program. In general, they should tell who is going to do what, when, how much, and how it will be measured. For example, if the collaborative's purpose or vision concerns the issue of teenage pregnancy, then the objective should include the reduction of teenage pregnancy, for example, "Seventy-five percent of the male participants will record an increase in knowledge concerning condom use skills by August 30, 2001." This is an impact objective that points to a decrease in the number of teenage pregnancies.

It is critical, however, to differentiate between means and ends, or methods and objectives. Usually, a community-developed collaborative is a means, not an end in and of itself. For example, an objective reading, "By December 1999, establish a teenage pregnancy prevention collaborative," might be an appropriate action step for a community organizer or facilitator, but it is an inappropriate objective because it does not address outcomes. What did the group do or change? The establishment of a new community group or the implementation of some activities does not necessarily indicate that a challenge was met or a problem was solved. The statement describes only the vehicle used to do something, not the thing that was done itself and the level of subsequent change achieved (whether positive or negative).

What will be the activities or the work done in the community by the group itself? Fawcett et al. (1984) call these *community actions*. Actions can be planned for by using action planning tools. Usually, these are divided into three areas: task(s) to be done, persons responsible, and date to be completed. A simple matrix that identifies these three components can achieve this purpose. An example is shown in Figure 9.3.

A vision is not the plan, but it paves the way for a plan and an implementation strategy that can be owned by gaining buy-in from the whole community because it was developed by the community. If this statement is true, then not only will the development of the coalition happen through the community, but also its activities will be implemented through the community as well.

STEP 4: DEVELOP GUIDING PRINCIPLES INCLUDING DECISION-MAKING AND ACTION TEAMS OR COMMITTEES

Everyone in the collaborative must know clearly who is making what decisions, when, and where. Problem solving and decision making are done by the appropriate work group or the community local work groups that have guidelines and policies to help them. Usually, the more responsibility taken by the smallest unit, the more productive and the more self-managing the community can become. The way the group works is best decided by the group itself. Group members decide their own procedures on the basis of the goals and direction of the organization, their particular areas of expertise, and their strengths and weaknesses. Early on in the group's formation, it will be important to make some agreements about the group's vision, mission, and how to act on objectives and action steps. On the basis of the agreements, group members develop a

Goal/Objective I

Goal: Continue facilitation of the DeKalb Tobacco Prevention Coalition.

Objective A: By February 28, 1997, identify at least five new community members to join in the efforts of the DeKalb Tobacco Prevention Coalition.

WORK PLAN

Task	Persons Responsible	Completion Date
• Speak with current DTPC members for contacts listing.	Jane Doe	December 31, 1996
• Call/arrange meeting with interested participants.	John Smith	January 31, 1997
• Identify and invite the new members to orientation whereby past, present, and future activities are discussed.	Jane Smith	February 28, 1997

Figure 9.3. Plan for Community Action

SOURCE: From *Work Group Evaluation Handbook: Evaluating and Supporting Community Initiatives for Health Development* (p. A1-16), by S. B. Fawcett, 1993, Lawrence, Kansas: Work Group on Health Promotion and Community Development. Reprinted with permission.

specific plan for collaborating and sharing accountability and leadership. For example, if the collaborative determines that it is important to develop community surveys and analyze the results, then it will need a partner with expertise in this area to conduct the analysis. A partner may bring expertise in the realm of evaluation. At a minimum, most groups wishing to conduct some evaluation of their work in communities will need to look for evaluation tools (to be discussed in Step 9).

How will the group decide who to invite or who will participate? There are many strategies for decision making. A few are as follows (not in any particular order): (a) vote—majority rule, (b) dictatorship—one decides for the group, (c) board or steering committee—arbitrator and decision maker, and (d) consensus—everyone is in agreement, which can be difficult to achieve without defining consensus as an approach that the majority supports and that others can live with. One clarifying question to ask can be, "Can anyone not live with this?"

Once operational guidelines are agreed on, then conflicts and impasses can be resolved or avoided altogether. The critical task here is how to include those who are traditionally excluded from decision making while, at the same time, making sure that they are included as full and equal partners.

Specific dialogue skills are needed to do this, as Martin's (1996) work in dialogue training illustrates. He suggests these guidelines for true dialogue to take place in groups:

> Listen to yourself and others; your internal disturbances, etc., welcome and encourage even disconfirming information such as different points of view, suspend certainties, focus on inquiry, speak for yourself, build on what is said, and listen to the silence. (p. 11)

Learning how the group makes decisions and how group members dialogue will be important for developing guiding principles. One specific system to develop these principles comes from Florin et al.'s (1995) efforts in identifying training and technical assistance needs in community coalitions. In this case, the example is a tool for establishing the level at which a coalition becomes operational with respect to *roles, structure,* and *functions.* For each of these three categories, the group will need a series of aspects to determine whether the work is complete or if work still needs to be done. To determine the roles that individuals/groups will play, six aspects are considered:

1. Develop policy about the type of representation expected of its members, individuals, or organization.

2. Develop written expectations for member participation.

3. Develop written descriptions of the responsibilities of officers.

4. Develop written descriptions of the responsibilities of subcommittee chairs.

5. Develop job descriptions for staff.

6. Develop balanced expectations for members/officers/staff/other participants in implementing activities.

The following seven aspects may be applied in considering the structure of the collaborative:

1. Define bylaws.

2. Develop an organizational chart.

3. Develop a committee structure to implement goals.

4. Develop a plan for membership selection and turnover.

5. Develop a plan for how leaders are selected and succeed one another.

6. Develop a standard orientation for new members.

7. Have written agendas at meetings and stick to them.

In assessing the level of functionality that the group has achieved at this point, the following points are helpful:

1. Develop a plan for how decisions will be made.
2. Establish an internal communication system.
3. Establish a system to communicate with various organizations and agencies.
4. Learn how to handle conflict.
5. Develop team spirit so that members are committed and involved and have a feeling of cohesiveness.
6. Increase knowledge skills in prevention and healthy communities through the following: identify areas that members want to know more about, distribute information and/or reading material, and plan training in prevention and other areas as needed.

Coalition ownership can be nurtured by rotating power, sharing power, or both. Control can rest with the group and not with the facilitator, or a steering committee can be convened. It is imperative that the structure of these committees reflects the particular needs and profile of the particular community. For example, a community composed of a large proportion of multiethnic cultural communities or neighborhoods can benefit from a committee focusing on translation, especially if inclusiveness is important to the collaborative. On the other hand, if the community is monocultural and all speak English, then a translation committee may not be high on a list of priorities.

Guidelines, in general, focus on process. How often will the collaborative meet? How long will the collaborative exist? What will be expected of participants, both as individuals and for those who represent stakeholders or large organizations, businesses, and corporations? These factors could also be considered as ground rules or rules for operation. For example, how will new members, participants, partners, and stakeholders become a part of the group? Can anyone visit collaborative meetings? Will collaborative and committee meetings be open to the public? How will new stakeholders and sponsors be approached? Who will be the lead agency or principal investigator for grants? Who has fiscal responsibility for the group? Will the newly formed collaborative apply for tax-exempt status, or will it be a for-profit entity? Some of these questions will need to be answered by the group early in its existence, whereas others will not need to be asked at all.

STEP 5: ANALYZE AND GAIN CONSENSUS ABOUT THE WORK TO BE DONE

At this step, it is assumed that the group has decided to use consensus as its decision-making methodology. Other assumptions at this stage include the following: Information has been collected for the group to review and consider (via a neutrally facilitated process), the group has the capacity or expertise to develop work teams or action teams, and the group has decided that a community-developed approach using coalition building is the strategy for change that their community needs. If indeed these assumptions are correct, the group is ready to engage Step 5 for the first time.

As a result of this step, the group may have decided to move forward through a coalition that will engage in a specific action. These actions may include an intervention strategy or a strategy for change to implement. For example, on the basis of information gained earlier in Step 1 (including epidemiological data), the group decides to address HIV/AIDS prevention. Via community assets mapping, the group determines what has been done in the community in the past to address the need and what the community's current capacity is to do anything about it now (see Step 6).

At this fifth step, another tool that has proved helpful is a *tactical gap analysis* (TGA) to compare where the collaborative/community is currently and where it would like to be in the future. This sounds like the visioning event mentioned earlier in Step 3; this is markedly different, however, in that the steps in getting from "A" to "B" are described as well. This includes a sequential order in which subsequent steps are dependant on prerequisites. Barry M. Kibel (1994), in his article "Evaluation of Local Prevention Processes: An Open-Systems Model in Action," describes a tactical gap analysis as follows:

> TGA is also a tool used to examine the maximum level of results anticipated for a project and as an assessment of project activities to ensure that their interim results will build to that level.
>
> If applied to the shift from the current operational model to the community health promotion paradigm, an anticipated process is as follows. One of the first steps is to include an analysis of the desired results of a fully operational community-developing (mobilizing) health education group. Maximum results to aim for might include the following results hierarchy:
>
> VI. *Outcome:* Reduction in number of problem incidents, change in behaviors
>
> V. *Impact:* Decision-making and actions less likely to contribute to the problem
>
> Gatekeepers: Community-at-large
>
> IV. *Environmental Shift:* Change in law, policy, resource allocation, program activity, or available options
>
> *Gatekeepers: Resource brokers and opinion shapers*
>
> III. *Action Preparation:* Dialogues conducted, key supporters and collaborators enlisted, plans developed, and resources mobilized
>
> *Gatekeepers: Colleagues and Supporters*

II. *Focusing:* Knowledge, skills, methods, strategies, and conceptual frameworks acquired for addressing the problem

Gatekeepers: Champions

I. *Motivation:* Attention drawn to a problem that needs to be addressed through prevention interventions

Gatekeepers: Advocates (p. 20)

These are listed in descending order to visualize how each level builds on the previous level.

Traditional health education programmatic results have been at levels I or II and, more recently, III or IV. Under the community organization and development paradigm, however, interest building and passive learning (I and II) are not going to develop coalitions for community organization and development. Examples of levels I and II activities include health fairs, classroom speaking, and community presentations. An enhancement or multiplier effect could be achieved in these areas, where awareness and publicity are important, if volunteers or graduate interns are trained and used by health educators to conduct these time-consuming, low-result activities. Examples of levels III and IV results and beyond include small grants programs, coalition building, and adoption of new practices. Usually, one or more activities will need to be modified to push the interim results to a higher level as described by the operational projection plans. Thus, it will be important for the coalition to decide not only what to aim for but also how to accomplish the steps necessary to arrive at it.

Strategies for Getting There: Interim Steps (A to B)

By using Program Evaluation and Review Techniques (PERT), a timetable that reflects the planning process held in juxtaposition to the organizational plan, one sees all the steps needed to have a team ready for implementation of community organization and development. Linking a tactical gap analysis (Kibel, 1994) that includes a PERT plan is a particularly helpful tool if the collaborative is applying for a grant or submitting a proposal. These tools can help the group plan which parts or components need to be in place by what time. An example of these interim steps, which are modifications of the community organization and development approach (Braithwaite et al., 1989), is shown below.[3] See also Figure 9.4.

Interim Steps	Date
1. Develop or modify goals and objectives, activities, evaluations, roles, and responsibilities	11/94
2. Identify communities with established contacts	11/94
3. Assess staff needs for coalition building and implementation	11/94

1	2	3	4	5	6	7	8	9	10	11	12
Nov	Dec	Jan	Feb	Mar	Apr	May	Jun	Jul	Aug	Sep	(+)

(1)

(2)→→→(5)→→→→→→→→(6)→→→→→→(7)→→(8)→→(10)→(11)→ (14)→→

(15)

(3) →→ (4)   (9)→→→→→→(12)

                                                                    (13)

Figure 9.4. Interim Steps
SOURCE: Braithwaite, Murphy, Lythcott, & Blumenthal (1989).

Interim Steps	Date
4. Inventory resources, research tools, and literature available	12/94
5. Identify or organize consortium/coalition groups within identified communities	12/94
6. Assess local community needs (focus groups)	3/95
7. Develop community health promotion and health education information packets	5/95
8. Organize coalition boards	6/95
9. Incorporate coalition board	6/95
10. Conduct local coalition community needs assessment	7/95
11. Conduct coalition forums	8/95
12. Plan health interventions	8/95
13. Provide continuing technical assistance	8/95
14. Conduct process and impact evaluations	9/95
15. Conduct outcome evaluations	(+)

STEP 6: MAP ASSETS/
BUILD RELATIONSHIPS

As mentioned earlier, the purpose of community assets mapping is to connect people with capacities (Kretzman & McKnight, 1993). There are three primary layers to community assets mappings: individuals, local associations, and local institutions.

Individual capacity inventories provide a snapshot of personal skills, interests, and experiences of individuals living in the community. The goal in a local

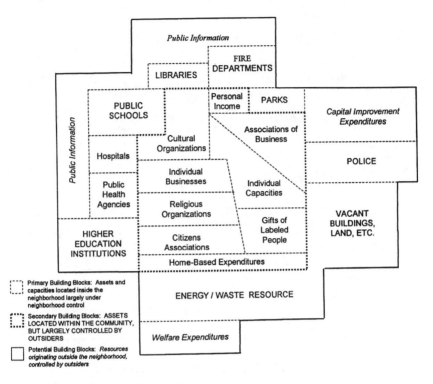

Figure 9.5. Neighborhood Assets Map

SOURCE: Adapted from McKnight & Kretzman (1990); used by permission.

associations inventory is to identify and catalog all the citizen-related groups that exist in the community and to subsequently generate a map (see Figure 9.5).

A map should be the result of assessing local institutions' facilities, materials, equipment, purchasing power, and so forth. Likely candidates include schools, businesses, police stations, faith institutions, and colleges. As public health practitioners, we know much about programming for a community's problems as opposed to its possibilities or capacity to do something. According to Kretzman and McKnight (1993), this is looking at the glass as half empty, rather than half full. In other words, needs assessments identify deficiencies that create images of needy people who require rescue from professionals. Community assets mapping, on the other hand, has advantages over the deficit model or needs assessments per se. These advantages include beginning with what is currently present in the community; looking to the community for solutions via agenda building and problem-solving capabilities of local institutions based on local guidance and control; and building relationships among those who live, work, and play in the community. An example of an inventory worksheet can be seen in Figure 9.6.

DeKalb County Board of Health
Division of Community Health Promotion

HIV/AIDS Prevention
Asset Mapping Survey/Questionnaire

1. Organization _____

2. Name: _____ 3. Position/Title: _____

4. Sex: M   or   F   5. Ethnicity: _____

5. Language(s) spoken: _____

6. How long in current position? _____

7. What experience has your organization had in HIV/AIDS primary prevention?

8. What types of prevention activities have you done?

9. What types of prevention activities do you like to do? What are your strengths?

10. How would you define the role of your group or organization in the community?

11. What are the major *long-term* goals of your group or organization?
    (What is the mission of your group?)

12. How would you describe the people who are involved in the mission of your
    organization? (demographics and characteristics?)

13. How many people are involved with the mission in your organization?

14. Who else would be working in primary prevention for HIV/AIDS in DeKalb County?

15. How do we contact them, and can we use your name as a reference?

16. Who do you believe are opinion makers or gatekeepers in primary prevention for
    HIV/AIDS in DeKalb County?

17. What barriers do you believe exist in primary prevention for HIV/AIDS in DeKalb
    County?

18. Who in the community needs to be involved to solve the problems of HIV/AIDS in
    DeKalb County?

Figure 9.6. Community Inventory Worksheets

19. In the future, would you be interested in doing any of the following:

_____ Serving on a coalition, task force, or committee

_____ Giving public endorsement or testimonial

_____ Donating resources such as a meeting place, advertising, staff time, etc.

_____ Conducting HIV 101 presentations in the community

20. How might you/your organization work with the CHP Division in the future?

Community Asset Tool

The Health Education staff thanks you for taking the time to complete this form. The results will be used to improve health promotion initiatives in your community.

Faith Community   (What is your zip code? _____)

1. What are you doing to help promote healthy behavior for your church members? *For example, health screenings, exercise programs, drug and alcohol classes*

What about for your community?

List groups working in the areas of prevention regarding teen pregnancy, substance abuse, etc.

2. Are your members active in community work?

May we have the names and phone numbers of church members interested in promoting good health?

Are you aware of anyone else in your area active in community work?

Community Asset Tool

The Health Education staff thanks you for taking the time to complete this form. The results will be used to improve health promotion initiatives in your community.

Business Groups   (What is your zip code? _____)

1. What are you doing in health promotion/prevention for your employees?
   For example, newsletters, employee wellness program

2. What volunteer activities are your employees involved in?

3. What kind of community-based activities have you sponsored?
   For example, job training programs, GED programs, school adoption

4. Do you donate office equipment? If so, what types?

5. What resources do you have for the community to use?
   For example, meeting rooms, food donations, free advertising

6. (Optional) Name _____ Phone number _____

(Continued)

Community Asset Tool

The Health Education staff thanks you for taking the time to complete this form. The results will be used to improve health promotion initiatives in your community.

Residents   (What is your zip code? _____)

1. What health resources are available in your community?
   Please provide the names of those resources.
   _____ Hospitals
   _____ Health maintenance organizations (HMOs)
   _____ Churches
   _____ Health centers
   _____ Recreation centers
   _____ Day care centers
   _____ Other _____

2. Where do you go for health services or health information?
   _____ Private doctor
   _____ Hospital
   _____ HMO
   _____ Community clinic
   _____ Health department
   _____ Other _____

3. Have you ever organized or participated in any of the following community activities?
   (Place a check mark if you have.)
   _____ Boy/Girl Scouts, Where _____
   _____ Church fundraiser, Where _____
   _____ Bingo, Where _____
   _____ School-parent associations, Where _____
   _____ Sports teams, Where _____
   _____ Camp trip for kids, Where _____
   _____ Field trips, Where _____
   _____ Political campaigns, Where _____
   _____ Block clubs, Where _____
   _____ Community groups, Where _____
   _____ Rummage sales, Where _____
   _____ Yard sales, Where_____
   _____ Church suppers, Where _____
   _____ Community gardens, Where _____
   _____ Neighborhood organizations, Where_____
   _____ Public speaking, Where_____
   _____ Other groups of community work, Where _____

4. Who are the leaders in your community?

5. What are the strengths of your neighborhood?
   For example, strong neighborhood watch program, block parties

6. (Optional) Name _____ Phone number _____

Figure 9.6. Continued

STEP 7: COMMUNICATE/SHARE INFORMATION

Similar to Kibel's (1994) description of mapping stories and their subsequent results, Stanley Hauerwas (1991) stresses in *A Community of Character* the importance of recording a community's narrative or story: "Such a community depends on the ability to trust in the gifts each brings to the group's shared existence" (p. 23). Thus, community is reinforced through sharing of stories (as well as what each person brings to the table). It helps bind the group together. Since antiquity, many communities have been sharing stories that define who they are. Likewise, it is critical for a community-organized and community-developed collaborative to communicate and share its narrative(s).

Communication, both external (media, newspapers, radio, television, etc.) and internal (collaborative members, stakeholders, facilitators, concerned citizens, etc.), ought to be consistent. The group needs to be clear about who talks with media and who speaks on behalf of the collaborative as opposed to speaking as a concerned citizen or as someone speaking for the school system or as someone who can address policy. This is really a megastep in that it ought to take place throughout all the steps or processes of the group's development. There should be no secrets. There may be committee meetings not open to the public, however, as well as stakeholder or steering committee communications that are specific to these groups. Proprietary information exists in any organization regardless of how formal or informal its structure. Tools for information sharing include agendas for meetings, minutes, focus groups, interviews, and other resources.

STEP 8: DO THE WORK

At this process step, the group does what it came together to do. This implementation phase includes acting on previously developed action steps and moving on them, communicating about them, and celebrating about them. On a programmatic level, the work can be divided into two domains. One is the formative work, or *community actions,* of the community group or collaborative itself; the second includes new changes that the group makes in the community per se, or *community changes* (Fawcett, 1993). Step 9 includes more about how to measure these. There are several strategies for community change that a coalition might consider, as well as typologies for prevention that they might select as vehicles for carrying out the work to be done.

Strategies for community change might include, but are not limited to, the following: (a) *popular education*—raising critical consequences of common concerns to increase knowledge (but alone it is not enough to create lasting community change); (b) *citizen participation*—involving citizens in policy planning and program implementation with an agency; (c) *mass mobilization*—amassing individuals and issues, for example, a community small grants program; (d) *social action*—building powerful organizations at the community level such as coalitions; (e) *public advocacy*—representing group interests in legislative, administrative, or other established institutional arenas (here the advocates activate themselves, rather than others); and (f) *local services development*—people providing their own services at the community level (if the burden is placed completely on the local community to modify its response, rather than on the society to modify the conditions that create the problems, however, this will only increase the service sector).

Similarly, types of prevention activities (Florin et al., 1995) from the afore-mentioned strategies could include but are not limited to the following:

- Increasing knowledge-raising awareness: mass media; special events to heighten awareness (e.g., health fairs, community forums, and class presentations)

- Building skills/competencies: refusal skills programs, parenting skills programs, decision-making and conflict management skills training

- Healthy alternative activities: support of youth athletic leagues, drop-in centers, school drug-free prom night activities

- Changing institutional or organizational policies: no tolerance of weapons on campus, policies concerning steroid use

- Law enforcement and regulatory practices: increased enforcement of underage tobacco use laws, efforts to remove cigarette dispensing machines, efforts to increase tobacco tax

- Building coalition/partnership capacity: efforts to increase the coalition's general viability and capacity to launch future activities (e.g., recruitment, advocating for additional funds, and seeking training and technical assistance)

- Building general institutional/community capacity: support of a parent-teacher association's fundraising effort, provision of technical assistance to a neighbor-hood association to map the assets of its community

Of course, other typologies of prevention work as well. This overview of activity categories, however, assists in the action planning that will provide the specific content for doing the work of prevention in the community. See Figure 9.7 for activities categories by prevention strategy.

STEP 9: PERFORM CONTINUOUS QUALITY IMPROVEMENT/PROCESS EVALUATION AS WELL AS IMPACT AND OUTCOME EVALUATION WHERE APPROPRIATE

Measuring the effectiveness of building coalition partnerships is in the midst of a major shift. Gone are the days of measuring coalitions by health status

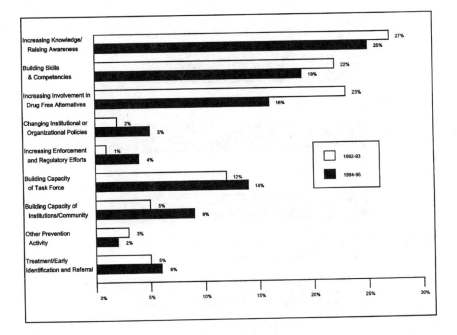

Figure 9.7. Profile of Task Forces' Activities Categorized by Prevention Strategies

outcomes alone, such as morbidity, mortality, incidence of disease, and teenage birthrates. Using strategies for measuring the products of the work done in community organization and development is critical to determining the level of success achieved and completing an accurate reflection of the work done. Informal groups simply keep notebooks of agendas and meeting minutes. More formal groups, wishing to develop long-term strategies, will want to identify and use measurement tools as well as community indicators and benchmarks. This level of participation will allow them to surpass process evaluation measurements only. Other measurements, such as respondents' perceptions of internal functioning (Florin et al., 1995), will be an invaluable measure for any group, as seen in Figure 9.8.

An indicator is simply the presentation of trends, whereas a benchmark is a specific measurement point to compare with other measurement points for accuracy (for example, how many gallons of milk are purchased from local stores each week during the summer). Indicators will need to be linked to the group's vision.

For any evaluation the collaborative uses, it is important to form working groups and to include local experts to assist the groups in measuring their efforts. Most indicators chosen will need to be small measurable sets of information that reflect the status of larger systems that show changes and

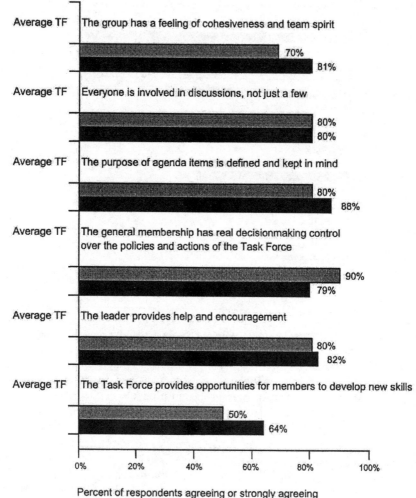

Figure 9.8. Perception of Task Force Internal Functioning

SOURCE: From *A Developmental Approach to Identifying Training and Technical Assistance Needs in Community Coalitions* (p. 13), by P. Florin, R. Mitchell, and J. Stevenson, May 1995. Paper presented at the National Conference on Health Promotion and Health Education, Atlanta, Georgia. Reprinted with permission.

trends through time. One critical qualifier to consider, however, is that in doing community organization and development, it is often difficult to initiate true experimental designs in a community. Therefore, it will be difficult to develop control groups in ethnically diverse areas (ethically, it may be difficult to justify). It would also be a difficult challenge to prove that specific community actions resulted in decreases in the number of teenage pregnancies within a particular census tract. On the other hand, the number of community actions that led to community changes that may have contributed to the ideal of decreased teenage pregnancies, based on or as evidenced by particular indicator shifts or changes, lends itself to recording all the work done. Once the data or results have been processed, it will be important to publicize and report the findings/results to the community at large.

As alluded to in the previous step, Fawcett (1993) and the Work Group on Health Promotion and Community Development at the University of Kansas have developed evaluation tools for capturing the process steps in developing community actions that led to community change (see Figure 9.9). Under this rubric, community actions are "actions taken in the community to bring about modified programs, policies, or practices," and community changes are "new or modified programs, policies, or practices in the community facilitated by the new initiative that reduces risks for problems targeted by the initiative" (p. 27). Examples of community actions include letters, phone calls, and town meetings. Examples of community changes include new or modified mentoring programs and entrepreneurial activities for prevention. Both these are activities outside planning meetings. They happen in the community per se, external to the collaborative itself. These two activities are helpful in designing the evaluation. If, on the other hand, only community actions were evaluated, success would be measured only by how the community was organized or how the strategy for change was implemented; thus, the evaluation would focus on whether the coalition was successfully formed. Measuring the community changes that occurred or what the coalition actually did, or "the what" that was done that made the difference in the community, points to replicability and sustainability of community-developed efforts for prevention.

Other steps for sustaining the effort implemented through these nine process steps for developing a coalition are also important. First, stage media events that highlight project achievements or goals as they are accomplished. Second, review action plans on a regular basis to see if tasks are being completed in a timely manner. Meet with action team chairs to review activities, and, if quantitative measures are not available, collect narratives that relate to the goals and accomplishments. Third, meet at least once a quarter with the larger planning group or coalition body to receive updates from the action team chairs.

Work continues to progress on how to close the gap between coalition work and health status outcomes. Fawcett et al. (1997) have worked with others to close this gap in the area of substance abuse prevention. Through their case studies of coalitions, greater resolution has been given to this issue.

Code	Definition	Examples
EXTERNAL EVENTS (Happens *outside* the initiative)		
CA Community Actions	Actions taken in the community to bring about a new or modified program, policy, or practice	• Letters • Phone calls • Town meetings
CC Community Changes	New or modified programs, policies, or practices in the community facilitated by the initiative that reduces risks for a problem targeted by the initiative	• A new (or modified) program (e.g., mentoring program • A new (or modified) policy (e.g., labeling low-fat foods) • A new (or modified) practice (e.g., regarding hours of service, or new collaboration)
SP Service Provided	Events that are designed to provide information, instruction, or develop skills of people in the community	• Classes • Workshops • Communications such as bill stuffers
M Media Coverage	Coverage of the initiative of its projects in the newspaper, radio, or television, or newsletter	• Radio • TV (e.g., PSAs) • Brochure
X Other	Items for which no code or definition has been created	• Phone calls to set up meetings • Internal staff meetings
INTERNAL EVENTS (Happens *within* the initiative)		
PP Planning Products	Results, or products of planning activities within the group	• Statements of objectives, or action plans developed • Formation of committees or task forces • Hiring new staff
RG Resources Generated	Acquisition of funding for the initiative through grants, donations, or gifts in kind	• Materials received • People's professional time • Money • Grants

Figure 9.9. Summary of the Observational Code for the University of Kansas Work Group's Community Evaluation System

SOURCE: From *Work Group Evaluation Handbook: Evaluating and Supporting Community Initiatives for Health Development* (p. A1-3), by S. B. Fawcett, 1993, Lawrence, Kansas: Work Group on Health Promotion and Community Development. Reprinted with permission.

RECAPITULATION OF NINE PROCESS STEPS

Coalition building is just one vehicle for implementing mass mobilization and social action strategies for change. Regardless of which model or combinations of models are used for community-developed approaches for prevention, the probability of failure increases significantly if it is not the entire community's work that closes the health gap. To be truly empowered, the community, regardless of the models and theories used, must have ownership of the initiative and be respected for its solutions. If not, the effort will be short-lived and will tend to cause more cynicism and foster mistrust between communities and institutions. Too often, the synergy between institutions, neighborhoods, and agencies is thwarted by organizations that round up the usual community suspects as partners simply because grant monies are available. Following these basic nine steps will help organize and mobilize a community's capacity for prevention. It is not a panacea, however. Working in the community context, from small grassroots neighborhoods to bureaucratic-regulated agencies, takes significant time and commitment for true collaboration toward community change that is sustainable, organized, and integrated into their systems.

Integration into systems will be necessary if an organization is going to give more than lip service to community coalition building. Lofquist's (1989) arenas of human service activity serve as an excellent tool for establishing framework and for describing where staff currently are in working with communities for prevention. The following matrix (see Figure 9.10) has proved helpful in assisting staff to focus their work to make changes as necessary. After staff have plotted their activities on the matrix, a summary can be generated. Aggregates for the participating staff can result in an indicator of staff readiness to engage in community organization and development. This integration is necessary for any organization planning on engaging in community organization and development where the work is with communities for prevention as opposed to individuals for remediation.

WHY COALITIONS FAIL

Community organizers and community coalition conveners should be aware of the typical reasons why coalitions fail. Some of these are listed below.

- *Turf issues.* Coalition members can become more invested in protecting their individual or organizational interests than in the development of the coalition as a whole. Selfish attitudes and a focus on individual agendas stunt the coalition's growth. A fixation on territorial protection works against the shared vision and common purpose of a community coalition.

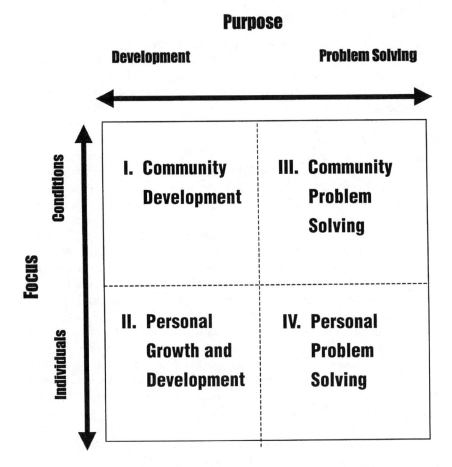

Figure 9.10. Arenas of Human Service Activity

SOURCE: From *The Technology of Prevention Workbook* (p. 7), by W. A. Lofquist, 1989, Tucson, Arizona: Development Publications. Copyright © by Development Publications. Reprinted with permission.

- *"I have the answer" attitude.* Members' advancing solutions to problems *before* the coalition has matured through a process is dangerous. Effective partnering acknowledges the importance of the group problem-solving process as opposed to one or a few individuals always having the answer. Although the answer that one individual offers may indeed be viable, the coalition can be undermined if one individual always offers the ideas in the absence of group process and void of consensus building.

- *Sabotage.* It is not uncommon for sabotage to prevail in coalitions in which members have competing priorities and no organized manner for reaching common ground and consensus. Sabotage is a strategy used to undermine a plan of action or approach decided on by some process. Some members can bring sour grapes to the table if their ideas failed to gain the support of the coalition members.

- *Interpersonal conflicts and long-standing feuds.* In many coalitions, members may have historical conflicts and long-standing feuds that debilitate and retard the growth potential of an emerging coalition. Effective leadership needs to be exerted in an effort to smoke out these annoyances for the common good of the coalition. When such interpersonal conflicts are surfaced, the involved members should be encouraged not to impose their personal baggage of conflicts on the coalition capacity-building process.

- *Lack of genuine inclusion.* No one likes to feel used in a pejorative sense. Thus, it is important to genuinely involve all coalition members in the planning, implementation, and evaluation of coalition activities. This is not a new observation. Community organizers have long known the pitfalls associated with the lack of inclusion (especially among recipient members) of members on the front end of decision-making processes.

- *Hidden agendas.* For obvious reasons, a hidden agenda can function to erode the common vision that a coalition seeks to implement. When someone has an ulterior motive that is self-serving, disruption and confusion will typically follow, akin to the problems associated with sabotage and protecting one's turf described above.

- *Lack of group ownership.* Ownership of the problem and the solutions has been discussed throughout this book. Many years ago, Stokely Carmichael advanced what has become the cliché, "If you are not part of the solution, you are part of the problem." Implied in this statement is the principle of ownership and that coalition members need to define, conceptualize, and identify their own problems in an effort to effect change and develop solutions.

- *Poor information/communication flow.* Within and among all organizations, communication and information flow are critical to effectiveness and goal attainment. Coalitions must address this issue head-on and have *a priori* protocols in place to resolve conflicts. For example, it should be clear who speaks for the coalition when media releases are an issue. Established reconciliation processes should also be in place when inevitable conflicts arise among coalition members relative to procedures or practice issues.

- *Lack of cultural competence.* Lack of cultural sensitivity when multiple ethnic or racial groups are involved with a coalition is a sure way to spell failure. Stereotyping and making demeaning or disparaging remarks about groups or classes of people will be offensive even to those who are thick-skinned. Cultural competence involves being genuine and being able to "walk in another person's shoes."

- *Poor leadership.* Poor leadership typically involves lack of good facilitation skills related to group processes. A good leader must also be a good follower. Thus, the ability to shift between the two roles is the sign of an effective leader.

- *Too many experts.* This is similar to the "I have the answer" syndrome noted above. Textbook strategies have their strengths and weaknesses. Simply because a strategy is in a textbook, however, does not mean it will work. Moreover, there is a time and place for the proper use of experts. Members should carefully assess when and where experts are to be employed. Although experts and/or recognized authorities should be involved at appropriate times, overuse and overreliance can undermine the expertise of community residents and other individual partners.

LESSONS LEARNED

Despite the reasons cited above for why coalitions fail, much has been learned in support of coalition maintenance and survival. Listed below are some of the ways to circumvent problems associated with coalition failure.

- *Know who you're getting in bed with.* Groups with historical feuds between them are typically not suited for strong partnering with each other. Such long-standing conflicts may be so deep-seated that resolution is impractical. Thus, when program announcements or other opportunities call for coalition partnerships among multiple organizations and community residents, one must be aware of the factor of partnering compatibility. Just as a couple requires compatibility for a successful relationship, so does a coalition. Although it is possible to have partners "kiss and make up" on long-standing issues of conflict, it is equally important to know the gravity of partners who will never work together amicably.

- *Use memoranda of agreement or memorandums of understanding.* When multiple organizations are involved with a newly forming coalition organization, it is advisable to use a memorandum of agreement or understanding as a nonlegal instrument to articulate principles that the partner members buy into. Such agreements are particularly useful when turnover occurs with agency or other representation on a coalition. The memorandum serves as a document to substantiate the agreements or understandings entered into by the earlier representative. This instrument is also valuable when government agency representatives change as a result of political shifts and changes.

- *Orient new members.* New members coming into a coalition should be properly oriented to the norms, values, and expectations of the coalition. A new member manual that includes pertinent information (bylaws, mission statement, roles and responsibilities, procedures, etc.) is crucial for the acculturation of new coalition members to the organizational ethos.

- *Recruit continually.* As has been discussed in previous chapters, the work of coalition building is stressful. Members may burn out after several months or years. Thus, recruitment should be viewed as a continual process of bringing "new blood" into the coalition. It is equally important to recruit different classes of new members, especially youthful members. The recruitment of high school students, for example, to serve on a primarily adult coalition is another means for developing leadership skills in the community.

- *Plan for conflict resolution.* Because conflict among coalition members, and even among those external to the coalition, is inevitable, it is prudent to have conflict resolution procedures in place. These measures will vary but could involve an executive committee decision-making protocol, a dispute resolution committee process, or other arbitration and mediation methods. The important point is to acknowledge that conflicts will arise and to have an established process for resolving them.

- *Acknowledge money as sugar and spice.* The introduction of money as a resource for coalitions to do projects can be viewed as both sugar and spice. It is sugar when resources are needed to implement needed initiatives, but such access sometimes brings participants out of the woodwork. This is true especially when grant money is involved, and everyone wants to play ball. The spice enters when the money is gone, and members begin to feel as if there no longer is an incentive for their involvement. The real and sustaining coalitions are the ones that stay organized after the money is gone.

- *Recognize member achievements.* It is crucial that the efforts of coalition members who solely volunteer their time be recognized. Keeping members motivated and participating regularly is a large enough task even when these individuals are compensated. A little well-deserved recognition is simply an approach to "stroking" people who need to know that their efforts are appreciated.

- *Conduct training and technical assistance.* All organizations have a need for member training and technical assistance. Such activities will be useful both in capacity building and in sustaining coalition leadership. (Suggested coalition training and technical assistance topics have been identified in the appendix.)

- *Plan strategically.* Coalitions must have a game plan. Such plans may involve both short- and long-term goals, but coalitions must plan their work and work their plan. Having a blueprint to guide the planning process is an essential activity for coalition sustenance.

- *Employ third-party evaluation.* Strong coalitions recognize the importance of having an independent evaluation of the coalition implementation activities. Such evaluative information is useful to funding sources and documents the accomplishments and the implementation problems needing redress.

NOTES

1. National Coalition for Healthy Cities and Communities: Hospital Research and Educational Trust/American Hospital Association, One North Franklin, Chicago, IL 60606 (312-422-2618).

2. In Florin, Mitchell, and Stevenson (1995), see their Tool for Task #2: Establishing Structure and Function.

3. See Braithwaite's (1992) chapter "Coalition Partnerships for Health Promotion and Empowerment" in *Health Issues in the Black Community* (Braithwaite & Taylor, 1992). In this rubric, the primary purpose of the community organization and development approach is to develop a health promotion and disease prevention model. Here, this model is a community-developed approach whereby the community identifies its health concerns, develops its prevention programs, forms its own decision-making mechanisms, and identifies resources for program implementation.

Appendix

Community Coalition Member Training
Needs Assessment Survey

Purpose

The purpose of this survey is to determine areas of needed training to enhance planning and coalition board effectiveness relative to the Center for Substance Abuse Prevention Community Partnership grant implementation.

Please circle whether you have *high* or *low* need for training in any of the following areas:

	Low		*Medium*		*High*
1. Strategic planning	1	2	3	4	5
2. Organizational development	1	2	3	4	5
3. Resource development	1	2	3	4	5
4. Leadership skills	1	2	3	4	5
5. Community problem solving	1	2	3	4	5
6. Project management	1	2	3	4	5
7. Fiscal management	1	2	3	4	5
8. Community organization	1	2	3	4	5
9. Coalition member recruitment strategies	1	2	3	4	5
10. Community health needs assessment surveys	1	2	3	4	5
11. Community mobilization strategies	1	2	3	4	5
12. Nonprofit incorporation	1	2	3	4	5

	Low		Medium		High
	Low		*Medium*		*High*
13. IRS tax-exempt status	1	2	3	4	5
14. Effective meeting management	1	2	3	4	5
15. Communication skills	1	2	3	4	5
16. Dealing with the media	1	2	3	4	5
17. Selecting/developing health interventions	1	2	3	4	5
18. Substance abuse prevention programs	1	2	3	4	5
19. Proposal development	1	2	3	4	5
20. Conflict resolution	1	2	3	4	5
21. Board-staff relationships	1	2	3	4	5
22. Program evaluation	1	2	3	4	5
23. Supervising staff personnel	1	2	3	4	5
24. Team building	1	2	3	4	5
25. Use of consultants	1	2	3	4	5
26. Obtaining technical assistance	1	2	3	4	5
27. Interpersonal communication	1	2	3	4	5
28. Short-range planning	1	2	3	4	5
29. Long-range planning	1	2	3	4	5
30. Program reporting	1	2	3	4	5
31. Program development	1	2	3	4	5
32. Newsletter development	1	2	3	4	5
33. Other _____	1	2	3	4	5
34. Other _____	1	2	3	4	5
35. Other _____	1	2	3	4	5

References

Adams, J. H. (1992). The mainstream environmental movement. *EPA Journal, 18*(1), 25-27.

Allen-Meares, P. (1989). Adolescent sexuality and premature parenthood: Role of the black church in prevention. *Journal of Social Work & Human Sexuality, 8,* 133-142.

Anderton, D. L., Anderson, A. B., Oakes, J. M., & Fraser, M. R. (1994). Environmental equity: The demographics of dumping. *Demography, 31*(2), 229-248.

Anderton, D. L., Anderson, A. B., Rossi, P. H., Oakes, J. M., Fraser, M. R., Weber, E. W., & Calabrese, E. J. (1994). Hazardous waste facilities: Environmental equity: Issues in metropolitan areas. *Evaluation Review, 18*(2), 123-139.

APEX-PH: Assessment protocol for excellence in public health. (1991). Washington, DC: National Association of County Health Officials.

Association of American Medical Colleges. (1997, October). *FACTS* (Monograph).

Axinn, J., & Levin, H. (1992). *Social welfare: A history of the American response to need.* White Plains, NY: Longman.

Bachtel, D. C., & Boatright, S. R. (Eds.). (1991). *The Georgia County guide.* Athens: University of Georgia Cooperative extension Service.

Bailey, C., Faupel, C. E., & Gundlach, J. H. (1993). Environmental politics in Alabama's black belt. In R. D. Bullard (Ed.), *Confronting environmental racism* (pp. 107-122). Boston: South End.

Battle, V. D. (1988). The influence of Al-Islam in America on the black community. *Black Scholar, 19,* 33-41.

Baugh, J. A. (1991). African-Americans and the environment: A review essay. *Policy Studies Journal, 19*(2), 182-191.

Bernstein, E., Wallerstein, N., Braithwaite, R., Gutierrez, L., Labonte, R., & Zimmerman, M. (1994). Empowerment forum: A dialogue between guest editorial board members. *Health Education Quarterly, 21*(3), 281-294.

Black church diabetes education program brings message of health. (1994, December 4). *California Voice,* p. 1.

Black church diabetes program gets underway in Los Angeles. (1994, September 22). *Los Angeles Sentinel,* p. A10.

Blackwell, J. E. (1991). *The black community: Diversity and unity* (3rd ed.). New York: HarperCollins.

Boatright, S. R., & Bachtel, D. C. (1998). *The Georgia County guide.* Athens, GA: University of Georgia Colleges of Agricultural & Environmental Sciences and Family & Consumer Services.

Bouie, J. (1993). *A community organization model for prevention of alcohol and other drug abuse, HIV transmission, and AIDS among African Americans.* Paper presented at the Second National Conference on Preventing and Treating Alcohol and Other Drug Abuse, HIV Infection, and AIDS in the Black Community: From Advocacy to Action, Rockville, MD.

Braithwaite, R. L. (1992). Coalition partnerships for health promotion and empowerment. In R. L. Braithwaite & S. E. Taylor (Eds.), *Health issues in the black community* (pp. 321-337). San Francisco: Jossey-Bass.

Braithwaite, R. L. (1994). Challenges to evaluation in rural coalitions [CSAP special issue]. *Journal of Community Psychology,* 188-200.

Braithwaite, R. L., Bianchi, C., & Taylor, S. E. (1994). An ethnographic approach to community organization and health empowerment. *Health Education Quarterly, 21*(3), 407-416.

Braithwaite, R. L., & Lythcott, N. (1989). Community empowerment as a strategy for health promotion for black and other minority populations. *Journal of American Medical Association, 261*(2), 282-283.

Braithwaite, R. L., Murphy, F., Lythcott, N., & Blumenthal, D. (1989). Community organization and development for health promotion within an urban black community: Conceptual model. *Health Education, 20*(5), 56-60.

Braithwaite, R. L., & Taylor, S. E. (Eds.). (1992). *Health issues in the black community.* San Francisco: Jossey-Bass.

Brown v. Board of Education, 347 U.S. 483 (1954).

Bryant, J. R. (1980). The black church as unifier of the black community. In L. S. Yearwood (Ed.), *Black organizations: Issues on survival techniques* (pp. 5-8). Washington, DC: University Press of America.

Bullard, R. D. (1992). Environmental blackmail in minority communities. In B. Bryant & P. Mohai (Eds.), *Race and the incidence of environmental hazards: A time for discourse* (pp. 82-95). Boulder, CO: Westview.

Bullard, R. D. (1994a). *Dumping in Dixie* (2nd ed.). Boulder, CO: Westview.

Bullard, R. D. (1994b). *People of color environmental groups directory, 1994-1995.* Atlanta, GA: Environmental Justice Resource Center.

Bullard, R. D. (Ed.). (1993). *Confronting environmental racism.* Boston: South End.

Butterfoss, F. D., Goodman, R. M., & Wandersman, A. (1993). Community coalitions for prevention and health promotion [Special issue: Community coalitions for health promotion]. *Health Education Research, 8*(3), 315.

Butterfoss, F. D., Goodman, R. M., & Wandersman, A. (1996). Community coalitions for prevention and health promotion: Factors predicting satisfactions, participation, and planning. *Health Education Quarterly, 23*(1), 65-79.

Butterfoss, F. D., Goodman, R. M., Wandersman, A., Valois, R. F., & Chinman, M. (1996). The plan quality index: An empowerment evaluation tool for measuring and improving the quality of plans. In D. Fetterman, S. Kaftarian, & A. Wandersman (Eds.), *Empowerment evaluation: Knowledge and tools for self-assessment and accountability* (pp. 304-331). Thousand Oaks, CA: Sage.

Capek, S. M. (1993). The "environmental justice" frame: A conceptual discussion and an application. *Social Problems, 40*(1), 5-24.

Centers for Disease Control and Prevention. (1993a). Cigarette smoking, attributable mortality and years of potential life loss, United States, 1990. *MMWR, 42*(33), 645-649.

Centers for Disease Control and Prevention. (1993b). Mortality trends for selected smoking-related cancers and breast cancer, United States, 1950-1990. *MMWR, 42*(44), 857-866.

Centers for Disease Control and Prevention. (1993c). Physician and other health-care professional counseling of smokers to quit, United States, 1991. *MMWR, 42*(44), 854-857.

Centers for Disease Control and Prevention. (1993d). *Planned approach to community change*. Atlanta, GA: Author.

Centers for Disease Control and Prevention. (1999, June 10). National Center for Chronic Disease Prevention and Health Promotion [On-line]. Available: http://www.cdc.gov/nccdphp/nccdphp.htm [1999, June 22].

Chavigny, K. H. (1988). Coalition building between medicine and nursing. *Nursing Economics, 6*(4), 179-183.

Chavis, D. M. (1995). Building community capacity to prevent violence through coalitions and partnerships. *Journal of Health Care for the Poor and Underserved, 6*(2), 234-245.

Chavis, D. M., Florin, P., & Felix, M. R. J. (1993). Nurturing grassroots initiatives for community development: The role of enabling systems. In T. Mizrahi & J. Morrison (Eds.), *Community and social administration: Advances, trends, and emerging principles*. New York: Haworth.

Chavis, D. M., Speer, P. W., Resnick, I., & Zippay, A. (1993). Building community capacity to address alcohol and drug abuse: Getting to the heart of the problem. In R. C. Davis, A. J. Lurigio, & D. Rosenbaum (Eds.), *Drugs and community*. Springfield, IL: Charles C Thomas.

Churches, blues, others help provide health care for uninsured children. (1994, September 13). *Michigan Chronicle*, p. 6A.

Cobb, A. T. (1991). Toward the study of organizational coalitions: Participant concerns and activities in a simulated organizational setting. *Human Relations, 44*(10), 1057-1079.

Cohen, L., Baer, N., & Satterwhite, P. (1991). Developing effective coalitions: An eight-step guide. *Injury Awareness & Prevention Centre News, 4*(10).

Collin, R. W., & Harris, W., Sr. (1993). Race and waste in two Virginia communities. In R. D. Bullard (Ed.), *Confronting environmental racism: Voices from the grassroots*. Boston: South End.

Davis, T. D., Bustamante, A., Brown, C. P., Wolde-Tsdik, G., Savage, E. W., Cheng, X., & Howland, L. (1994). The urban church and cancer control: A source of social influence in minority communities. *Public Health Reports, 109,* 500-506.

Day, P. J. (1997). *A new history of social welfare.* Boston: Allyn & Bacon.

DePue, J. D., Wells, B. L., Lasater, T. M., & Carleton, R. A. (1987). Training volunteers to conduct heart health programs in churches. *American Journal of Preventive Medicine, 3,* 51-57.

Dluhy, M. J. (1984). Moving from professionalism to political advocacy in the human services: How to organize a successful statewide political effort in youth services. *Journal of Sociology and Social Welfare, 11*(3), 654-683.

Dluhy, M. J. (1990). *Building coalitions in human services.* Newbury Park, CA: Sage.

Du Bois, W. E. B. (1907). *Economic cooperation among Negro Americans.* Atlanta, GA: Atlanta University Press.

Eagles, C. W. (1986). *The civil rights movement in America.* Jackson: University Press of Mississippi.

Edwards, C. H. (1990). An ecological model for prevention of drug use. In U. J. Dyemade & D. Brandon-Monye (Eds.), *Ecology of alcohol and other drug use: Helping black high risk youth* (OSAP Monograph 7, pp. 35-44). Rockville, MD: U.S. Department of Health and Human Services, Public Health Service, Alcohol, Drug Abuse, and Mental Health Administration, Office for Substance Abuse Prevention.

Eisen, V. A. (1994). Survey of neighborhood-based comprehensive community empowerment initiatives [Special issue: Community empowerment, participatory education]. *Health Education Quarterly, 21*(2), 235-252.

Ellison, B. (1994, January 18). White House report: More black health care providers needed. *Philadelphia Tribune,* p. 2A.

Eng, E., & Hatch, J. W. (1991). Networking between agencies and black churches: The lay health advisor model. *Prevention in Human Services, 10,* 123-146.

Eng, E., Hatch, J. W., & Callan, A. (1985). Institutionalizing social support through the church and into the community. *Health Education Quarterly, 12,* 81-92.

Environmental Protection Agency. (1992a). Environmental protection: Has it been fair? *EPA Journal, 18*(1), 18-22.

Environmental Protection Agency. (1992b). *Respiratory health effects of passive smoking: Lung cancer and other disorders.* Washington, DC: U.S. Environmental Protection Agency, Office of Research and Development, Office of Air and Radiation.

Environmental Protection Agency. (1995a). *Environmental justice 1994 annual report: Focusing on environmental protection for all people* (EPA-200-R-95-003). Cincinnati, OH: National Center for Environmental Publications and Information.

Environmental Protection Agency. (1995b). *Environmental justice strategy: Executive Order 12898* (EPA-200-R-95-002). Cincinnati, OH: National Center for Environmental Publications and Information.

Estell, K. (1994). *Reference library of black America* (Vol. 4). Detroit, MI: Gale Research.

Fawcett, S. B. (1993). *Work group evaluation handbook: Evaluating and supporting community initiatives for health development.* Lawrence, KS: Work Group on Health Promotion and Community Development.

Fawcett, S. B., Lewis, R. K., Paine-Andrews, A., Francisco, V. T., Ritcher, K. P., Williams, E. L., & Copple, B. (1997). Evaluating community coalitions for prevention of substance abuse: The case of project freedom. *Health Education & Behavior,* 2(6), 812-828.

Fawcett, S. B., Paine-Andrews, A., Francisco, V. T., Schultz, J. A., Richter, K. P., Lewis, R. K., Williams, E. L., Harris, K. J., Berkley, J. Y., Fisher, J. L., & Lopez, C. M. (1995). Using empowerment theory in collaborative partnerships for community health and development. *American Journal of Community Psychology, 23*(5), 677-697.

Fawcett, S. B., Seekins, T., Whang, P. L., Muiu, C., & Suarez de Balcazar, Y. (1984). Creating and using social technologies for community empowerment. *Prevention in Human Services, 3,* 145-171.

Flexner, A. (1910). *Medical education in the United States and Canada: A report to the Carnegie Foundation for the Advancement of Teaching.* New York: Carnegie Foundation.

Florin, P., Mitchell, R., & Stevenson, J. (1995, May). *A developmental approach to identifying training and technical assistance needs in community coalitions.* Paper presented at the National Conference on Health Promotion and Health Education, Atlanta, GA.

Ford Foundation. (1994). *Current interests of the Ford Foundation: 1994 and 1995.* New York: Author.

Foundation Center. (1993). *Guide to U.S. foundations, their trustees, officers, and donors.* New York: Author.

Francisco, V. T., Paine, A. L., & Fawcett, S. B. (1993). A methodology for monitoring and evaluating community health coalitions. *Health Education Research, 8,* 403-416.

Frazier, E. F. (1963). *The Negro church in America.* New York: Vintage.

Freudenberg, N. (1984). *Not in our backyards!* New York: Monthly Review Press.

Fulton County Health Department. (1995). *Annual report.* Atlanta, GA: Author.

Gamson, W. (1961). A theory of coalition formation. *American Sociological Review, 26,* 373-382.

Gerstein, D. R., & Green, L. W. (Eds.). (1993). *Preventing drug abuse: What do we know?* Washington, DC: National Academy Press.

Gilliam, A. (1992). Homeless women with children. In R. L. Braithwaite & S. E. Taylor (Eds.), *Health issues in the black community.* San Francisco: Jossey-Bass.

Goeppinger, J. (1993). Health promotion for rural populations: Partnership interventions. *Family & Community Health, 16*(1), 1-10.

Goodman, R. M., & Wandersman, A. (1994). FORECAST: A formative approach to evaluating community coalitions and community-based initiatives [CSAP special issue]. *Journal of Community Psychology,* 6-25.

Goodman, R. M., Wandersman, A., Chinman, M., Imm, P., & Morrissey, E. (1996). An ecological assessment of community-based interventions for prevention and health promotion: Approaches to measuring community coalitions. *American Journal of Community Psychology, 24*(1), 33-61.

Gottlieb, N. H., Brink, S. G., & Gingiss, P. L. (1993). Correlates of coalition effectiveness. *Health Education Research, 8*(3), 375-384.

Haber, D. (1983). Promoting mutual help groups among older persons. *Gerontologist, 23,* 251-253.

Haines, H. H. (1988). *Black radicals and the civil rights mainstream, 1954-1970.* Knoxville: University of Tennessee Press.

Hatch, J. W., & Jackson, C. (1981, May). North Carolina Baptist Church Program. *Urban Health,* 70-71.

Hatch, J. W., & Lovelace, K. A. (1980). Involving the southern rural church and students of the health professions in health education. *Public Health Reports, 95,* 23-25.

Hauerwas, S. (1991). *A community of character.* Notre Dame, IN: University of Notre Dame Press.

Herman, K. A., Wolfson, M., & Forster, J. L. (1993). The evolution, operation and future of Minnesota SAFPLAN: A coalition for family planning. *Health Education Research: Theory & Practice, 8*(3), 331-344.

Himmelman, A. (1994). Collaboration for a change: Definitions, models, and roles, with a user-friendly guide to collaborative processes from the authors: Communities working collaboratively for a change [Adapted version]. In M. Hermann (Ed.), *Resolving conflict: Strategies for local government* (pp. 27-47). Washington, DC: International City/County Management Association.

Holman, P., Jenkins, W. C., Gayle, J. Q., Carlton, D., & Lindsey, B. K. (1991). Increasing the involvement of national and regional racial and ethnic minority organizations in HIV information and education. *Public Health Reports, 106*(6), 687-694.

Hunt, G. P. (1994). Ethnography and the pursuit of culture: The use of ethnography in evaluating the community partnership program [CSAP special issue]. *Journal of Community Psychology,* 52-60.

Jacques, G. (1992). *The African-American movement today.* New York: African-American Experience.

Jellinek, P. S., & Hearn, R. P. (1991). Fighting drug abuse at the local level. *Issues in Science and Technology, 8,* 78-84.

Johnson, K. (1993). Health care coalitions: An emerging force for change. *Hospital & Health Services Administration, 38*(4), 557-571.

Johnson, K., Grossman, W., & Cassidy, A. (Eds.). (1996). *Collaborating to improve community health: Workbook and guide to best practices in creating healthier communities and populations.* San Francisco: Jossey-Bass.

Johnson, O. S. (1980). The social welfare role of the black church. *Dissertation Abstracts International, 41*(05), 2293A. (University Microfilms No. DEM80-24554)

Join Together. (1993). *Community leaders speak out against substance abuse.* Boston: Robert Wood Johnson Foundation.

Joint Task Force of the National Association of Community Health Centers and the National Rural Health Association. (1989). *Journal of Public Health Policy, 10*(1), 99-116.

Jones, J. H. (1993). *Bad blood: The Tuskegee syphilis experiment.* New York: Free Press.

Jones, S. (1991). Fundraising: Developing and using the advisory board. *Nurse Educator, 16*(4), 36, 37, 39.

Kaftarian, S. J., & Hansen, W. B. (1994). Improving methodologies for the evaluation of community-based substance abuse prevention programs [CSAP special issue]. *Journal of Community Psychology,* 3-5.

Karger, H., & Stoesz, D. (1990). *American social welfare policy: A structural approach.* New York: Longman.

Katz, W. L. (1969). *The American Negro: His history and literature.* New York: Arno/ New York Times.

Kennedy, J., & Riley, P. (1986, December). The future of coalitions. *Business and Health, 4,* 30-31.

Kibel, B. M. (1994, Summer). Evaluation of local prevention processes: An open-systems model in action. *New Designs, 1,* 15-22.

Kim, S., Crutchfield, C., Williams, C., & Hepler, N. (1994). An innovative and unconventional approach to program evaluation in the field of substance abuse prevention: A threshold-gating approach using single system evaluation designs [CSAP special issue]. *Journal of Community Psychology,* 61-78.

Kong, B. W., Miller, J. M., & Smoot, R. T. (1982). Churches as high blood pressure control centers. *Journal of the National Medical Association, 74,* 920-923.

Kretzman, J. P., & McKnight, J. L. (1993). *Building communities from the inside out: A path toward finding and mobilizing a community's assets.* Evanston, IL: Center for Urban Affairs and Policy Research.

Kumanyika, S. K., & Charleston, J. B. (1992). Lose weight and win: A church-based weight loss program for blood pressure control among black women. *Patient Education and Counseling, 19,* 19-32.

Lasater, T. M., Wells, B. L., Carleton, R. A., & Elder, J. P. (1986). The role of churches in disease prevention research studies. *Public Health Reports, 101,* 125-131.

Lavelle, M., & Coyle, M. (1992, September 21). Unequal protection: The racial divide in environmental law. *National Law Journal, 15,* 1-2.

Lee, C. (1992). Toxic waste and race in the United States. In B. Bryant & P. Mohai (Eds.), *Race and the incidence of environmental hazards: A time for discourse* (pp. 10-27). Boulder, CO: Westview.

Lee, C. (1993). Beyond toxic waste and race. In R. D. Bullard (Ed.), *Confronting environmental racism* (pp. 41-52). Boston: South End.

Levin, J. S. (1984). The role of the black church in community medicine. *Journal of the National Medical Association, 76,* 477-483.

Levin, J. S., & Taylor, R. J. (1993). Gender and age differences in religiosity among black Americans. *Gerontologist, 33,* 16-23.

Lincoln, C. E., & Mamiya, L. H. (1990). *The black church in the African American experience.* Durham, NC: Duke University Press.

Lofquist, W. A. (1989). *The technology of prevention workbook.* Tucson, AZ: Associates for Youth Development/Development Publications.

Mansergh, G., Rohrach, L. A., Montgomery, S. B., Pentz, M. A., & Johnson, C. A. (1996). Process evaluation of community coalitions for alcohol and other drug abuse prevention: A case study of comparisons of researcher- and community-initiated models. *Journal of Community Psychology, 24,* 118-135.

Martin, D. (1996, April). *Dialogue training.* Paper presented at the Community Council for a Healthier De Kalb, Atlanta, GA.

McAdoo, H., & Crawford, V. (1990). The black church and family support programs. *Prevention in Human Services, 9,* 193-203.

McCloud, A. B. (1995). *African American Islam.* New York: Routledge.

McCollum, M. J. (1994, June 3). Black clergy protests outdoor cigarette ads. *Philadelphia Tribune,* p. 2A.

McKissack, F., & McKissack, P. (1991). *The civil rights movement in America.* Chicago: Children's Press.

McKnight, J., & Kretzman, J. (1990). *Mapping community capacity.* Evanston, IL: Northwestern University, Center for Urban Affairs and Policy Research.

McLaughlin, C. G., Zellers, W. K., & Brown, L. D. (1989). Health care coalitions: Characteristics, activities, and prospects. *Inquiry, 26,* 72-83.

McLeRoy, K. R., Kegler, M., Steckler, A., Burdine, J. M., & Wisotzky, M. (1994). Community coalitions for health promotion: Summary and further reflections [Editorial]. *Health Education Research, 9,* 1-10.

McMillan, B., Florin, P., Stevenson, J., Kerman, B., & Mitchell, R. E. (1995). Empowerment praxis in community coalitions. *American Journal of Community Psychology, 23*(5), 699-727.

Mohai, P., & Bryant, B. (1992). Environmental racism: Reviewing the evidence. In B. Bryant & P. Mohai (Eds.), *Race and the incidence of environmental hazards: A time for discourse.* Boulder, CO: Westview.

Morris, A. D. (1984). *The origins of the civil rights movement: Black communities organizing for change.* New York: Free Press.

Morrison, J. D. (1991). The black church as a support system for black elderly. *Journal of Gerontological Social Work, 17,* 105-120.

Mosher, J. F. (1992). Alcohol and poverty. In S. E. Samuels & M. D. Smith (Eds.), *Improving the health of the poor* (pp. 97-121). Menlo Park, CA: Henry J. Kaiser Family Foundation.

Nager, N., & Saadatmand, F. (1991). The status of medical education for black Americans. *Journal of the National Medical Association, 83*(9), 787-792.

National Association for Equal Opportunity in Higher Education. (1988). *Institutional and presidential profiles of NAFEO's 117 historically black colleges and universities.* Washington, DC: Author.

National Cancer Institute, Division of Cancer Prevention and Control. (1991). *America stop smoking intervention study, training manual: Coalition problem solving.* Bethesda, MD: Author.

National Center for Health Statistics. (1993a). Advanced report on final mortality statistics, 1991. *Monthly Vital Statistics Report (Supplement), 42*(2).

National Center for Health Statistics. (1993b). *Health, United States, 1992* (DHHS Publication No. PHS 93-1232). Washington, DC: Government Printing Office.

National Institute on Drug Abuse. (1988). *Drug abuse warning network.* Washington, DC: National Institute on Drug Abuse Press Office.

National Institute on Drug Abuse. (1990). *National household survey on drug abuse: Highlights, 1988* (DHHS Publication No. ADM 90-1682). Washington, DC: National Institute on Drug Abuse Press Office.

Neighbors, H. W., Braithwaite, R. L., & Thompson, E. (1995). Health promotion and African Americans: From personal empowerment to community action. *American Journal of Health Promotion, 9*(4), 281-287.

Office of Minority Health. (1995). *Office of Minority Health profile.* Rockville, MD: U.S. Department of Health and Human Services.

Olson, L. M., Reis, J., Murphy, L., & Gehm, J. H. (1988). The religious community as a partner in health care. *Journal of Community Health, 13,* 249-257.

Perrine, M., Peck, R., & Fell, J. (1989). Epidemiologic perspectives on drunk driving. *Surgeon General's workshop on drunk driving: Background papers.* Washington, DC: U.S. Department of Health and Human Services, Public Health Service.

Perry, E. J. (1981, May). The Memphis church-based high blood pressure program. *Urban Health,* 69-70.

Phoenix, J. (1993). Getting the lead out of the community. In R. D. Bullard (Ed.), *Confronting environmental racism* (pp. 77-92). Boston: South End.

Plessy v. Ferguson, 163 U.S. 537 (1896), 165 Ct. 1138, 41 L.Ed.

Prothrow-Stith, D., & Weissman, M. (1991). *Deadly consequences.* New York: Harper-Collins.

Putnam, R. (1994, August). *Bowling alone: Democracy in America at the end of the twentieth century.* Paper presented at the Nobel Symposium "Democracy's Victory and Crisis," Uppsala, Sweden.

Reagon, B. J. (1983). Coalition politics: Turning the century. In B. Smith (Ed.), *Home girls: A black feminist anthology* (pp. 356-368). New York: Kitchen Table: Women of Color Press.

Rees, F. (1991). *How to lead work teams.* San Diego, CA: Pfeiffer.

Robinson, R. G., Pertschuk, M., & Sutton, C. (1992). Smoking and African Americans. In S. E. Samuels & M. D. Smith (Eds.), *Improving the health of the poor* (pp. 123-181). Menlo Park, CA: Henry J. Kaiser Family Foundation.

Robinson, W. S. (1978). *International library of Afro-American life and history: Historical Afro-American biographies.* Cornwell Heights, PA: Publishers Agency.

Rock, C. B. (1996). *Perspectives black Seventh Day Adventists face in the twenty-first century.* Hagerstown, MD: Review & Herald Publishing.

Rogers, T., Howard-Pitney, B., Feighery, E. G., Altman, D. G., Endres, J. M., & Roeseler, A. G. (1993). Characteristics and participant perceptions of tobacco control coalitions in California. *Health Education Research: Theory & Practice, 8*(3), 345-358.

Roper, W. L., Baker, E. L., Dyal, W. W., & Nicola, R. M. (1992). Strengthening the public health system. *Public Health Reports, 107*(6), 609-615.

Rowland, D., & Lyons, B. (1989). Triple jeopardy: Rural, poor, and uninsured. *Health Services Research, 23,* 875-1004.

Rubin, R. H., Billingsley, A., & Caldwell, C. H. (1994). The role of the black church in working with black adolescents. *Adolescence, 29,* 251-266.

Russell, K. (1992). Strengthening black and minority community coalitions for health policy action. *Journal of the National Black Nurses Association, 6*(1), 42-47.

Scarlett, M. E., Williams, K. R., Kenneth, R., & Cotton, M. F. (1991). A private organization and public agency partnership in community health education. *Public Health Reports, 106*(6), 667-671.

Seabrook, C. (1998, March 8). The body snatchers of Augusta. *Atlanta Journal Constitution,* pp. C1, C4.

Sherwood, R. W., Porcher, F. K., & Hess, J. W. (1993). Promoting rural primary care practices: A partnership planning model. *Family & Community Health, 16*(1), 67-72.

Smith, D. B. (1990). Population ecology and the racial integration of hospitals and nursing homes in the United States. *Milbank Quarterly, 68*(4), 561-597.

Smith, S. R., & Lipsky, M. (1993). *Nonprofits for hire: The welfare state in the age of contracting.* Cambridge, MA: Harvard University Press.

Staggenborg, S. (1986). Coalition work in the pro-choice movement: Organizational and environmental opportunities and obstacles. *Social Problems, 33*(5), 374-390.

Stephens, T., Braithwaite, R. L., & Taylor, S. E. (1998). Model for using hip-hop music for small group HIV/AIDS prevention counseling with African American adolescents and youth adults. *Patient Education and Counseling, 35,* 127-137.

Stern, L. (1991, September). Coalitions: The convergence continues. *Business and Health, 9,* 8-17.

Stevenson, W., Pearce, J., & Porter, L. (1985). The concept of "coalition" in organization theory and research. *Academy of Management Review, 10*(2), 256-268.

Stewart, K., & Klitzner, M. (1993). How well do national programs take account of local situations? Case studies of comprehensive community planning to address alcohol and other drug issues: The evaluation of the Fighting Back Initiative. In T. K. Greenfield & R. Zimmerman (Eds.), *Experiences with community action projects: New research in the prevention of alcohol and other drug problems* (CSAP Prevention Monograph 14). Rockville, MD: U.S. Department of Health and Human Services, Public Health Service, Substance Abuse and Mental Health Services Administration, Center for Substance Abuse and Prevention.

Summerville, J. (1983). *Educating black doctors: A history of Meharry Medical College.* University: University of Alabama Press.

Tackling youth violence: Celebrating Christmas. (1992, December 5). *Richmond Afro-American,* B4.

Taravella, S. (1992, March 16). Black hospitals' fortunes, ranks still declining. *Modern Health Care, 22*(11), 56-57.

Taylor, D. (1989). Blacks and the environment: Toward an explanation of the concern and action gap between blacks and whites. *Environment and Behavior, 21*(2), 175-205.

Taylor, D. (1992). The environmental justice movement: No shortage of minority volunteers. *EPA Journal, 18*(1), 23-25.

Taylor, D. (1993). Environmentalism and the politics of inclusion. In R. D. Bullard (Ed.), *Confronting environmental racism* (pp. 53-62). Boston: South End.

Thomas, S. B., & Quinn, S. C. (1993). The burdens of race and history on black Americans' attitudes toward needle exchange policy to prevent HIV disease. *Journal of Public Health Policy, 14,* 320-347.

Thomas, S. B., Quinn, S. C., Billingsley, A., & Caldwell, C. (1994). The characteristics of northern black churches with community health outreach programs. *American Journal of Public Health, 84,* 575-579.

Thompson, B., Wallack, L., Lichtenstein, E., & Pechacek, T. (1990-1991). Principles of community organization and partnership for smoking cessation in the community intervention trial for smoking cessation (COMMIT). *International Quarterly of Community Health Education, 11*(3), 187-203.

Trattner, W. I. (1989). *From poor law to welfare state: A history of social welfare in America.* New York: Free Press.

Tuckson, R. V. (1989). Race, sex, economics, and tobacco advertising. *Journal of the National Medical Association, 81*(11), 1119-1124.

Tuggle, M. B. (1995). New insights and challenges about churches as intervention sites to reach the African-American community with health information. *Journal of the National Medical Association, 87*(Suppl. 8), 635-637.

Tushnet, M. V. (1987). *The NAACP's legal strategy against segregated education, 1925-1950.* Chapel Hill: University of North Carolina Press.

United Church of Christ Commission for Racial Justice. (1987). *Toxic waste and race in the United States: A national report on the racial and socioeconomic characteristics of communities with hazardous waste sites.* New York: United Church of Christ.

U.S. Bureau of the Census. (1992). *Table 34: U.S. physicians by Hispanic origin and race by sex, EEO files for 1980 and 1990.* Washington, DC: Author.

U.S. Congress. (1994). *Environmental justice: Hearings before the Subcommittee on Civil and Constitutional Rights of the House Committee on the Judiciary,* 103d Cong., 1st Sess. (March 3-4, 1993). Washington, DC: Government Printing Office.

U.S. Department of Commerce, Bureau of the Census, and U.S. Department of Health and Human Services, National Institutes of Health, National Institute on Aging. (1993). *Profiles of America's elderly: Racial and ethnic diversity of America's elderly population* (POP/93-1). Washington, DC: Government Printing Office.

U.S. Department of Health and Human Services. (1985). *Report of the secretary's task force on black and minority health* (Vol. 1, Executive Summary). Washington, DC: Government Printing Office.

U.S. Department of Health and Human Services. (1988). *The health consequences of smoking: A report of the surgeon general* (DHHS Publication No. CDC 88-8406). Washington, DC: Author.

U.S. Department of Health and Human Services. (1989). *Reducing the health consequences of smoking: 25 years of progress* (DHHS Publication No. CDC 89-8411). Washington, DC: Author.

U.S. Department of Health and Human Services. (1994a). *Healthy people 2000 review, 1993* (DHHS Publication No. DHHS 94-1232-1). Washington, DC: Author.

U.S. Department of Health and Human Services. (1994b). *National household survey on drug abuse: Population estimates* (DHHS Publication No. SMA 95-3063). Washington, DC: Author.

U.S. Department of Health and Human Services. (1994c). *Preventing tobacco use among young people: A report of the surgeon general* (DHHS Publication No. 95-0110-P). Washington, DC: Author.

U.S. Department of Health and Human Services. (1994d). *Signs of effectiveness II: Preventing alcohol, tobacco, and other drug use: A risk factor/resiliency-based approach* (S. E. Gardner, P. F. Green, & C. Marcus, Eds.). Rockville, MD: U.S. Department of Health and Human Services, Public Health Service, Center for Substance Abuse Prevention.

U.S. Department of Health and Human Services. (1995a). *The community prevention coalitions demonstration grant program.* Rockville, MD: U.S. Department of Health and Human Services, Public Health Service, Center for Substance Abuse Prevention.

U.S. Department of Health and Human Services. (1995b). *Prevention: 1993 and 1994 federal programs and progress: Healthy People 2000.* Rockville, MD: U.S. Department of Health and Human Services, Public Health Service, Office of Disease Prevention and Health Promotion.

U.S. General Accounting Office. (1988). *Siting of hazardous waste landfills and their correlation with racial and economic status of surrounding communities.* Washington, DC: Author.

U.S. General Accounting Office. (1995a). *Hazardous and nonhazardous waste: Demographics of people living near waste facilities.* Washington, DC: Author.

U.S. General Accounting Office. (1995b). *10 studies on demographics near waste facilities.* Washington, DC: Author.

U.S. Government Printing Office. (1992). *Linking medical education and training to rural America: Obstacles and opportunities* [Workshop by the Special Committee on Army, U.S. Senate, 102d Cong., 1st Sess., July 29, 1991]. Washington, DC: Author. (Serial No. 102-8)

Wandersman, A., Valois, R., Ochs, L., de la Cruz, D. S., Adkins, E., & Goodman, R. M. (1996). Toward a social ecology of community coalitions. *American Journal of Health Promotion, 10*(4), 299-307.

Whigham-Desir, M. (1994). Will black doctors win or lose in health reform? *Black Enterprise, 24*(12), 70-78.

Wiist, W. H., & Flack, J. M. (1990). A church-based cholesterol education program. *Public Health Reports, 105,* 381-388.

Williams, C., Jr., & Williams, H. B. (1984). Contemporary voluntary associations in the urban black church: The development of growth of mutual aid societies. *Journal of Voluntary Action Research, 13*(4), 19-30.

Woodson, C. G. (1934). *The Negro professional man and the community.* Washington, DC: Association for the Study of Negro Life and History.

World Book. (1995). *World book encyclopedia.* Chicago: Author.

World Health Organization. (1989). *Guide to planning health promotion for AIDS prevention and control* (WHO AIDS Series No. 5). Washington, DC: Author.

Index

About the Authors

Ronald L. Braithwaite is Professor of Behavioral Sciences and Health Education at the Rollins School of Public Health of Emory University and is Adjunct Professor in the Department of Community Health and Preventive Medicine at Morehouse School of Medicine, where he formerly directed a health promotion resource center. He received his B.A. and M.S. degrees from Southern Illinois University in sociology and rehabilitation, respectively. He received his Ph.D. degree from Michigan State University in educational psychology in 1974. He has done postdoctoral studies at Howard University, Yale University, and the University of Michigan School of Public Health and Institute for Social Research. Using several contemporary models for program evaluation, he has evaluated education, health, and human service programs. He has taught research design, statistics, program evaluation, testing and measurement, community organization, and minority health at the graduate level to nursing, medical, and public health students. He is widely published in education and health journals and is coeditor of *Health Issues in the Black Community* (1992) and *Prison and AIDS: A Public Health Challenge* (1996). His work in community organization and development has gained national attention, and he has consulted for numerous federal, state, and private organizations. He has also served as principal investigator for a formative evaluation of HIV/AIDS education and prevention programs in correctional settings, funded by the Centers for Disease Control and Prevention and the Association of Schools of Public Health. Currently, he serves as principal investigator for a community-based public health practice partnership funded by the Health Resources and Services Administration and an HIV intervention project for juvenile detainees in the Georgia Boot Camps funded by NIAAA.

Sandra E. Taylor is Associate Professor in the W. E. B. Du Bois Department of Sociology at Clark Atlanta University. She received her B.A. (1977) from Norfolk State University, her M.A. (1978) from Atlanta University, and her Ph.D. (1983) from Washington University. She has done postdoctoral studies at the University of Michigan and has studied abroad in the former East and West Germany and in parts of West Africa. Her most recent publications are on health and illness with a specific focus on HIV/AIDS. She is coeditor of *Health Issues in the Black Community* (1992). Her current research interests are in coalition formation for HIV/AIDS prevention and evaluation of health promotion programs for minority youth. She has held research appointments with the Nell Hodgson School of Nursing and the Rollins School of Public Health of Emory University and currently heads the affiliate site at Clark Atlanta University of the Southeastern AIDS Training and Education Center (SEATAC) of the Emory University School of Medicine. She has served as a consultant for various government and private sector initiatives and serves on the advisory boards of several health-related organizations.

John N. Austin is Professor and Department Chair for the Social Work Program at Delaware State University. He received his B.A. (1973) in political science, his M.S.W. (1974) with an emphasis in community organization and social planning from Virginia Commonwealth University (VCU), and his Ph.D. (1984) in research, policy, and administration from the School of Social Work at VCU. Formerly, he was Professor of Social Work at Norfolk State University and served on the faculty at Longwood College and Hampton University. He has consulted for numerous educational, mental health, and human service agencies including federal agencies and foundations and has been active in providing technical assistance and training to community-based organizations and coalitions throughout the United States.